NEW
WEBSTER'S

LAW
FOR
EVERYONE

Edited by
Hugo Sonnenschein,
LL.B., LL.M., J.D.

AVENEL BOOKS · NEW YORK

CONTENTS

INTRODUCTION

The law touches almost every aspect of modern life. Every worker has certain legal rights regarding his employment and certain responsibilities he must fulfill. In buying a home, a car, or a toy for a child, each person has certain rights that are guaranteed to him. Whether driving to work, moving to another state, or traveling to a foreign country, the citizen is protected by the law. In order to function effectively in modern society, each citizen needs a basic understanding of his rights and responsibilities before the law.

The laws of the United States of America have a dual foundation. The Constitution provides an outline of the rights guaranteed to every citizen. The common law establishes, in a large measure, the rules and regulations under which we live. The *common law* is a body of law and jurisprudence that was originated, developed, and formulated in England prior to the settlement of North America. It has become the basis of the law in most of the United States. The common law records legal decisions that serve as precedents to be followed in cases of the same general nature.

From this foundation the law is constantly changing, growing to meet the needs of an expanding society. Laws may be changed in two ways: by statute, or by court decision. A legislature may pass new laws, called *statutes*, to deal with modern problems. Workmen's compensation, social security, and antitrust laws were created in this way. Or, where statutes or legal precedents do not offer clear guidelines, the court makes its decision by interpreting the earlier law to fit a new situation.

In cases involving similar facts, of course, the courts are bound by precedents, and the lower courts are bound by decisions of the higher courts. The federal courts in a particular state must follow the decisions of the supreme and appellate courts of that state, except in cases involving the interpretation of the Constitution and laws of the United States or on questions that are purely procedural. The courts in one state are not bound by the decisions of a court in another state. Of course a common law decision may be set aside by statute, or modified when it no longer applies to present conditions.

There are four main classes of courts in each of the states. The first are the courts that have jurisdiction over petty criminal offenses and in which minor suits are brought. Second, there are the courts of general jurisdiction, in which more important suits are brought. Next are the appellate courts, and finally there is the state supreme court, or court of last resort, which reviews decisions of lower courts.

Of course, the judicial system varies widely in the different states. For example, the 1971 Constitution of the State of Illinois provides that "the judicial power is vested in a Supreme Court, an Appellate Court, and Circuit Courts. Circuit Courts ... have original jurisdiction of all judicial matters except where the Supreme Court has original and exclusive jurisdiction ...." The larger counties of the state divide the circuit court into various divisions—chancery, criminal, county, divorce, juvenile, laws and probate—to hear special types of cases. Cities over a certain size have municipal courts with jurisdiction over cases confined to the city.

There are three classes of federal courts. The lowest is called the District Court, taking its name from the fact that the country as a whole is divided into districts, with one court for each district. Next is the Circuit Court of Appeals, to which appeals from the District Court are taken. And finally, there is the United States Supreme Court, in which appeals may be sought from decisions of the courts of appeal, of the supreme courts of the several states and, in certain criminal cases, directly from decisions of the Federal District Courts.

Upon application made in proper form, an appeals court decides whether or not it will review a particular case. A court will review the decision of a lower court only if the application is founded on errors in the former proceedings. For example, the proof of wrongful admission of evidence or of refusal to admit proper evidence in the former trial would be sufficient to obtain a hearing.

Evidence includes all means and ways by which the truth of an alleged fact is established or disproved. *Direct evidence* is the testimony of a witness or of written documents and records that are competent, relevant, and material to issues joined and that, if believed, prove the existence of the fact in issue without any inference. *Circumstantial evidence* is a chain of facts or circumstances, all tending, when connected, to establish a logical inference or conclusion that such a fact does exist.

The difference between civil and criminal law is not always understood. *Criminal law* may be defined as the law dealing with offenses against the people as a whole. The acts that are crimes are clearly defined by statute, and the cases are prosecuted by public officers. *Civil law* covers laws dealing with wrongs against an individual or a group. Wrongful acts may be subject to both criminal and civil actions. If a man steals an automobile, he has committed a crime against the state; at the same time the person robbed may bring civil action against him for the loss. See CRIMINAL LAW; TORTS.

The two terms *law* and *equity* are also frequently misunderstood. The word *law* signifies a rule of action, either written or unwritten. *Equity* looks to the substance rather than to the form. When an act is equitable it may be just, even though it has no foundation in the law. Formerly, separate courts existed to try cases in equity, but the modern tendency is to combine law and equity and to give judges the power to try both law and equity cases. See EQUITABLE REMEDIES; LEGAL REMEDIES.

New Webster's Law for Everyone includes information on such recent legal developments as job discrimination, consumer protection, and truth in advertising. In addition, it defines and clarifies traditional legal concepts. Unfamiliar legal terms are defined in the text, and a glossary explains some of the more frequently used terms.

New Webster's Law for Everyone is not intended to provide the reader with enough knowledge to act as his own lawyer—the law is far too complex for that. But the editors have made every effort to explain basic legal ideas concisely and clearly, so that layman will have a better understanding of his rights and obligations under the law.

LAW FOR THE LAYMAN

Acknowledgment

1. DEFINITION—An *acknowledgment* is a statement sworn in the presence of a proper authority that a certain document is the free and voluntary act of the person making the acknowledgment. All chattel mortgages and all documents relating to or affecting real estate—such as deeds, mortgages, and releases—must be acknowledged.

2. WHO MAY TAKE ACKNOWLEDGMENTS—Notaries public, justices of the peace, masters in chancery, and judges and clerks of courts of record are authorized to take acknowledgments in most cases. The official attaches a *certificate of acknowledgment* to the document.

3. SPECIAL CASES—The laws of some states require the acknowledgment to show, in cases where an instrument is signed by both husband and wife, that the wife signed out of the presence of her husband. Many states also require that an acknowledgment taken before a notary public must show the date his commission expires. See NOTARIES PUBLIC: ACKNOWLEDGMENTS.

4. FORMS—These forms are commonly used for certificates of acknowledgment.

CHATTEL MORTGAGE

STATE OF ILLINOIS,)
KANE COUNTY.   )ss.

I, John Richard, a Justice of the Peace in the Town of Dundee, in and for the said County, do hereby certify that this mortgage was duly acknowledged before me by the above named........................,
the grantor therein named, and entered by me this 17th day of July, 19 . ...

    Witness my hand and seal.
      (Seal)

                JOHN RICHARD
                Justice of the Peace

RELEASE

STATE OF ILLINOIS,   )
COUNTY OF DU PAGE.)ss.

    I, John Smith, a Notary Public in and for said County, and in the State aforesaid, do hereby certify that **James Y. Scammon**, who is personally known to me to be the same person whose name is subscribed to the foregoing instrument, appeared before me this day in person and acknowledged that he signed, sealed, and delivered the said instrument as his free and voluntary act for the uses and purposes therein set forth.

    Given under my hand and Notarial Seal this 13th day of May,19 . . . . .

    (Notarial Seal)

                         JOHN SMITH
                         Notary Public

MORTGAGES AND DEEDS

STATE OF ILLINOIS,   )
COUNTY OF DU PAGE)ss.

    I, John Smith, a Notary Public in and for said County in the State aforesaid, do hereby certify that **Samuel P. Smith and Sarah E. Smith**, his wife, who are personally known to me to be the same persons whose names are subscribed to the foregoing instruments, appeared before me this day in person and acknowledged that they signed, sealed, and delivered said instrument as their free and voluntary act for the uses and purposes therein set forth, including a release and waiver of all rights under and by virtue of the homestead exemption laws of this State.

    Given under my hand and Notarial Seal this first day of January, A.D. 19 . . . . .

    (Notarial Seal)

                         JOHN SMITH
                         Notary Public

GENERAL AND SHORT FORM

STATE OF ILLINOIS,)
COUNTY OF COOK.)ss.

    On the . . . . day of . . . . in the year one thousand nine hundred and . . . ., before me personally came (names of both parties), who are known to me to be the individuals described in, and who executed, the foregoing instrument, and acknowledged that they executed the same.

                    (Signature)

Affidavits

1. DEFINITIONS—An *affidavit* is a voluntary statement of fact reduced to writing and sworn to or affirmed before an authorized public officer. An affidavit is not admissible as testimony in a court of law because the maker, or *affiant*, cannot be cross-examined, but a person who makes a false affidavit may be punished for perjury.

2. FORM—The following is a common form, which, with certain modifications, can be made to apply to most cases.

AFFIDAVIT

STATE OF ILLINOIS,)
COUNTY OF COOK.)ss.

John Jones being duly sworn on his oath states that he is well acquainted with the handwriting of Daniel Seitz, one of the subscribing witnesses to the deed hereto attached; that affiant has frequently seen him write and knows his signature; that he believes that the name of the said Daniel Seitz, signed in the said deed, is in the handwriting of the said Daniel Seitz, and further affiant says not.

> (Signed)
> JOHN JONES

Subscribed and sworn to before me this 28th day of February, A.D. 19 . . . .

> (Notarial Seal)

> E. M. SCHWARTZ
> Notary Public

Agency

1. DEFINITIONS—*Agency* is the relationship between two or more persons by which the *agent* represents the *principal* in the transaction of lawful acts or business. Agents are of two kinds, general and special. A *general agent* is authorized to represent the principal in all of his business, or in all business of a particular kind. A *special agent* is authorized to do a specific thing, such as sell a farm, buy a house, or transact some special business for the principal.

2. PRINCIPAL AND AGENT—Any person who is legally able to act for himself may act as principal. This excludes a lunatic, an alien enemy, or any other person incapable of contracting. On the other hand, any person who is of sound mind and understanding may act as an agent. Husband and wife may act for each other except where prevented by the statutes of the particular state. A person unable to contract on his own account, such as a person under age, may some-

times act as an agent. Anyone except a lunatic, imbecile, or infant of tender years may be an agent. Corporations often act as agents.

3. AUTHORITY, HOW GIVEN—The authority of an agent may be constituted in three ways: by deed under seal, by writing, or merely by word. Express authority is given to an agent by what is called a *power of attorney*. If the authority is to execute a writing under seal and acknowledged, the power of attorney must be likewise under seal and acknowledged. In a few states, however, this rule has been changed by statute. An agent to sell land or to do any other important business where he is required to make contracts or to draw or sign notes, drafts, or checks, should be appointed by a carefully drawn legal document. Agency may be implied from previous dealings and transactions between the parties. If the principal has held a person out as an agent he will be bound by his acts, even though as a matter of fact the agent had no express authority to represent him.

4. AGENT'S RESPONSIBILITY—The agent must obey the instructions of his principal and act in good faith, using all necessary care and skill in conducting agency business. He cannot appoint a substitute or delegate his authority to another without consent of his principal. An agent concealing the identity of his principal is himself responsible and, if acting fraudulently or deceitfully, is himself responsible to third parties. If an agent embezzles his principal's property, it may be reclaimed if it can be identified or distinctly traced. An agent employed to sell property cannot buy it himself; an agent employed to purchase property cannot buy from himself.

5. PRINCIPAL'S LIABILITY—The principal is liable for all acts of his agent within the scope of the agency. Also, the knowledge of the agent relating to the business of the agency is binding upon the principal; therefore, notice to an agent as to matters relating to the agency is notice to the principal. The principal is liable to third persons for the negligence or unskillfulness of the agent acting in the fulfillment of the agency business, although money mistakenly paid by an agent can be recovered by the principal. Any acts or contracts of an agent made beyond the scope of his authority may be ratified by the principal and when so ratified are binding on the latter. The general rule with respect to the liability of a principal for unauthorized acts of his agent is that the principal is liable to third persons for any acts done by the agent for the principal in the course of his duties and within the actual or apparent scope of his agency.

6. REVOCATION OF AUTHORITY—The authority of an agent may be terminated in seven ways: (a) by the express revocation thereof by the principal, (b) by renunciation of such power by the agent, (c) by the death of the principal, (d) by the expiration of the time within which the agent was to perform the acts that were to be done by him, or by his having completed and fully performed the commission and closed the business which he was to transact, (e) by the sale of the subject matter of the agency, (f) by the insanity of either principal or agent, or (g) by the bankruptcy of the principal or the agent. A revocation of authority takes effect, insofar as the agent is concerned, when he receives notice thereof; insofar as the third persons are concerned, when they receive notice of such revocation. Personal notice or its equivalent is required, and is sufficient, to those who have dealt with the agent. Advertising the fact would be sufficient as to all others. Without a sufficient notice of the revocation, a contract made in good faith with the agent after a revocation will bind the principal the same as before. However, incapacity or death of either party terminates the agency even without notice.

7. SPECIAL RULES OF AGENCY—An agent cannot delegate his powers to another without the consent of the principal, unless the act to be done is a minor service, or one requiring no personal ability or skill. Both principal and agent are liable if the persons with whom the agent is transacting business do not know of the agency relationship. An agent can receive no personal profit from a transaction.

8. DEALING THROUGH AN AGENT—Persons dealing with agents who are strangers should be very careful to ascertain that the agent has authority to transact business in hand. In all transactions in regard to real estate, the authority of the agent should be in writing, signed by the owner of the property, in order to be binding upon the owner. In all cases of doubt as to the authority of an agent or as to the extent of his authority, it would be wise to require of the agent a written proof of his agency and the extent of his authority.

9. POWER OF ATTORNEY—Whenever it becomes necessary to delegate to an agent the power to sign notes, checks, or other legal documents, it is advisable to grant such powers in a written document. Such document is usually called a *power of attorney*. It should be signed by the principal and witnessed, and should set forth exactly and explicitly what the attorney or agent has power to do. If the agent is to deal in real estate it is sometimes required by law, and in any event always advisable, that such power of attorney be under seal.

10. FORMS:

POWER OF ATTORNEY, GENERAL FORM

Know all men by these presents, That I, James L. Binton, of Naperville, County of Du Page, and State of Illinois, have made, constituted and appointed, and by these presents do make, constitute and appoint, Chas. A. Lerch true and lawful attorney for me and in my name, place and stead, (here state the purpose for which the power is given), giving and granting unto my said attorney full power and authority to do and perform all and every act and thing whatsoever, requisite and necessary to be done in and about the premises, as fully, to all intents and purposes, as I might or could do if personally present, with all power of substitution and revocation, hereby ratifying and confirming all that my said attorney or his substitute shall lawfully do or cause to be done by virtue thereof.

In witness whereof, I have hereunto set my hand and seal the 2nd day of January, one thousand nine hundred...................

Signed, Sealed and Delivered
  in Presence of

....

JAMES L. BINTON (Seal)

Note: This form should be properly acknowledged before an officer, the same as a deed according to the law of the State.

PROXY OR POWER OF ATTORNEY TO VOTE

Know all men by these presents: That I, David E. Hughes, do hereby constitute and appoint C. A. Brown my true and lawful attorney, for me and in my name, place and stead, to vote as my proxy and representative at the .... meeting of the stockholders of the ...., a corporation, and at any adjournment of said meeting, all of the .... shares of the capital stock of said corporation standing in my name on the books of said corporation, as fully and amply as I could or might do were I personally present; with full power of substitution and revocation.

Witness my hand and seal at Aurora, Illinois, this 26th day of June, A.D. 19 ....

E. R. ZEMMER (Seal)

REVOCATION OF POWER OF ATTORNEY

Whereas, I, Sylvester Jones, of Aurora, County of Kane, and State of Illinois, did on the tenth day of June, 19 . . . . ., by my letter or power of attorney appoint John C. Cook of Chicago my true and lawful attorney, for me and in my name to (here state in precise language what he was authorized to do) as by the said power of attorney, reference thereunto being had, will fully appear;

Therefore, know all men by these presents, That I, Sylvester Jones, aforesaid, have revoked and recalled the said power of attorney, and by these presents do revoke and recall all power and authority thereby given to the said John C. Cook.

Given this tenth day of October, 19 . . . .

Signed and sealed in presence

of . . . .

SYLVESTER JONES (Seal)

Antitrust Law

1. DEFINITION—A *trust* is a corporation or conglomerate having monopolistic power within its field of commerce. Various laws have been passed to prevent such combinations from using unfair methods of competition. The federal antitrust laws are the Sherman Act, the Clayton Act, the Federal Trade Commission Act, and the Robinson-Patman Act. The Sherman Act is concerned with agreements in restraint of trade and actual and attempted monopolization of markets. The Clayton and Federal Trade Commission Acts are concerned with anticompetitive exclusive dealing arrangements and mergers and with unfair methods of competition. The Robinson-Patman Act is concerned with discriminatory pricing and promotions in the distribution of goods.

2. HISTORY OF THE SHERMAN ACT—Through various conspiratorial and predatory practices, numerous monopolies had emerged in the United States by 1890 in such diverse industries as whiskey, petroleum, sugar, cotton, oil, and lead. They were called *trusts* because competing companies were typically combined in restraint of trade by transferring controlling stock interests in them to a board of trustees for integrated noncompetitive operation. Soon the "holding company" corporation replaced the trust as the device used.

3. PASSAGE OF THE SHERMAN ACT—To break up these monopolies, combinations, and conspiracies, Congress

passed the Sherman Act. Under Section 1 of that act, "Every contract, combination in the form of trust or otherwise, or conspiracy, in restraint of trade or commerce among the several states, or with foreign nations, is declared to be illegal...."

4. THE COURT CONSTRUES THE SHERMAN ACT—In 1911 in the Standard Oil and American Tobacco cases the United States Supreme Court held that against its common law background the Sherman Act must be read to forbid only "contracts or acts" having a "monopolistic tendency," and hence only unreasonable restraints of interstate or foreign commerce; that is, any undue interference with freely competitive markets. Under this "rule of reason" the Court will consider economic evidence to determine whether a restrictive agreement unduly hampers competition.

5. RESTRAINTS OF TRADE UNREASONABLE PER SE — Beginning with Standard Oil, however, the Court has declared certain forms of conduct to be violations of the statute per se—that is, such restraints are unreasonable as a matter of law "because of their pernicious effect on competition and lack of any redeeming virtue"—and no economic evidence will be received "as to the precise harm they caused or the business excuse for their use." Forming the core of regulations under Section 1, the principal "per se categories" are agreements between competitors to fix prices, to limit production, to divide markets or customers, or to boycott other businessmen.

a. *Price Fixing*. A seller may not agree horizontally with his competitors on the price at which they will sell, or vertically with his customers on their resale prices; whether or not the participants have power to control the market price, or such prices are "reasonable" or yield only a "reasonable profit," or are minimums designed to preserve a product's quality image, or are maximums intended to insure competitive resale price levels or to prevent overcharging.

b. *Production Limitations*. Agreements of suppliers to limit their production affect fundamental supply and demand relationships and are automatically outlawed.

c. *Market Division*. Suppliers are not allowed to divide the market even if necessary to avoid "ruinous competition" among themselves or to compete with the larger national chain stores.

d. *Tying Arrangements*. Tying arrangements condition the sale of one product, the "tying" product, on the purchase of another, the "tied" product, from the same seller. For example, a manufacturer of a popular brand of cold cream might decide to sell that product only to retailers who purchase a certain quota of the manufacturer's lipstick. The cold cream would be the "tying" product, the lipstick the "tied" product. The tying arrangement would permit the manufacturer to boost sales of lipstick even though his competitors might offer a better product. Such arrangements are bad per se "whenever a party has sufficient economic power with respect to the tying product to appreciably restrain free competition in the market for the tied product."

6. REASONABLE RESTRAINTS OF TRADE —Outside of these per se categories the rule of reason will support restraints of trade that serve legitimate business goals and are not seriously anticompetitive. Covenants, reasonable in time and space, forbidding the seller of a business from competing with the buyer, and covenants granting exclusive franchises within a shopping center, are two examples of reasonable restraints.

7. CONSPIRACY OR COMBINATION—So little is needed to support a finding of agreement or conspiracy that competitors should not discuss subjects on which they could not legally agree, for example, setting prices or refusing to deal with third parties, for such a discussion followed by parallel action will support a finding of commitment to a common plan.

8. MONOPOLIZATION—Section 2 of the Sherman Act makes it unlawful to "monopolize, or attempt to monopolize, or combine or conspire with any other person or persons, to monopolize any part of" the interstate or foreign commerce of the United States.

9. HISTORY OF THE CLAYTON ACT—The Clayton Act was passed in 1914 during President Wilson's first term. The statute reflected the general sentiment that the Sherman Act standing alone was inadequate to guarantee free competition, partly because the Sherman Act dealt with accomplished restraints, as distinguished from incipient abuses. Consequently, among other things, the Clayton Act forbids exclusive dealing and certain mergers where the effect may substantially lessen competition or tend to create a monopoly. The Federal Trade Commission may halt incipient restraints through its power to forbid unfair methods of competition in interstate commerce.

10. EXCLUSIVE DEALING—Section 3 of the Clayton Act forbids any interstate supplier to sell commodities on the condition that the buyer will not use or deal in the goods of a firm competing with the seller. This law applies to any case where the exclusive dealing may substantially lessen com-

petition in any line of commerce.

11. MERGERS—Section 7 of the Clayton Act forbids the acquisition of all or any part of the stock or assets of a corporation doing an interstate business "where in any line of commerce in any section of the country, the effect of such acquisition may be substantially to lessen competition or tend to create a monopoly." The statute regulates mergers between competing corporations ("horizontal"), between corporations in a supplier-customer relationship ("vertical"), and all other mergers ("conglomerate") where reasonably probable anticompetitive effects are shown.

12. PRICE DISCRIMINATION—The original price discrimination provisions of the Clayton Act were intended principally to prevent interstate sellers from lowering prices to destroy local competitors while maintaining prices elsewhere. With the advent of retail chains, the statute had proved inadequate to prevent the chains from exacting from sellers discriminatory prices and related concessions through the use of their superior purchasing power. Since they could pay lower prices for their merchandise, retail chains could sell at lower prices and drive smaller retail stores out of the market.

13. ROBINSON-PATMAN ACT—As amended in 1936 by the Robinson-Patman Act, Section 2(a) of the Clayton Act broadens the law to prohibit price discrimination that gives unfair advantage either to the seller, as in the case of a chain store lowering prices in one part of the country to destroy competition there, or to the buyer, as in the case of a chain store demanding price reductions from its supplier, or to the customers of the seller or the buyer.

14. GOVERNMENT ENFORCEMENT OF CIVIL REMEDIES — Violations may be restrained by injunctions and by administrative cease-and-desist orders ranging from a simple prohibition of price fixing to broad orders limiting specific business practices that, in and of themselves, would not have been antitrust violations. A civil penalty of up to $5,000 is provided for each violation of a final cease-and-desist order issued by the FTC, with each day's noncompliance constituting a separate violation.

15. PRIVATE ENFORCEMENT OF CIVIL REMEDIES—Section 4 of the Clayton Act provides that "any person who shall be injured in his business or property by reason of anything forbidden in the antitrust laws shall recover three fold [sic] the damages by him sustained, and the cost of suit, including a reasonable attorney's fee."

Auctioneer

1. DEFINITION—An *auctioneer* is a person employed to sell property to the highest bidder at public sale.

2. AGENT FOR BOTH BUYER AND SELLER—An auctioneer is the exclusive agent of the owner until the auctioneer accepts the purchaser's bid and knocks down the property to him. On accepting the bid the auctioneer becomes the agent of the purchaser also, and thus represents both parties.

3. COMPLETION OF THE SALE—A sale by auction is completed when the auctioneer announces its completion by the fall of the hammer, or in any other customary manner. Until such announcement is made, the auctioneer may withdraw the property from sale unless the sale has been advertised to be without reserve. Any bidder may also withdraw his bid at any time before the fall of the hammer.

4. RESPONSIBILITY OF AUCTIONEER—Authority to sell property does not imply power to sell at auction. Thus a purchaser buying goods from an auctioneer, when he knows the auctioneer has no authority to sell them at auction, acquires no title to the property thus purchased. The seller or owner is not bound by any statements by the auctioneer. An auctioneer must accept the most favorable bid. He cannot refuse to accept legitimate bids, but he is justified in rejecting the bids of insane or drunken persons, minors, trustees of the property, and persons who refuse to comply with the terms of the sale.

5. THINGS AN AUCTIONEER CANNOT DO—An auctioneer is not permitted to delegate his duties to another, except minor or incidental duties. He cannot act contrary to the wishes and instructions of the owners in any matters relating to the details of the sale. He may not permit a bidder to withdraw his bid after its acceptance, without the consent of the owner. He cannot sell the property to himself or employ another to bid for him. He is not permitted to sell at private sale contrary to the owner's instructions.

Automobile

1. THE RIGHT TO USE THE HIGHWAYS—The public has a right to use the public roads to travel and transport property. Drivers of automobiles have an equal right on the highways with other vehicles, but they do not have any greater right. The courts hold that all travelers have equal right to use the highways. Thus, a pedestrian has the same right as the driver of an automobile. The state cannot exclude nonresidents from the public roads or place greater restrictions or burdens on nonresident motorists than those imposed on

its own citizens.

2. PARKING—In the absence of any city ordinance or statutory regulation, an automobile may be left at the side of the road with the engine shut off and the brakes set. However, an automobile so left after dark must be properly lighted.

3. LICENSE—The several states issue licenses to the owners of automobiles, motorcycles, and trucks, permitting them to use the public highways. Many cities require a municipal license. Such a license is neither a contract nor a tax, but a *statutory entitlement* that may be revoked only through due process of law. The license does not pass to a purchaser of the vehicle.

4. RENTED VEHICLES—The owner of a rented vehicle is not liable for the negligence of the operator. For example, if A rents his automobile to B for a certain consideration, the law will not hold A responsible for the negligent acts of B even if B is an unskilled driver. On the other hand, if A knew when he rented the car that B was an immature child or a person of low mentality or under the influence of alcohol, the courts would hold him responsible. If the owner lends his car with a chauffeur, he will be held liable for the negligent acts of the chauffeur. In case of damage to the rented car, the renter is liable only if it can be proved that he did not exercise ordinary prudence and care. Should the renter sell the car without the owner's authority, the owner can recover even from an innocent purchaser. The owner of an automobile is entitled to a fair compensation for its use, even if no definite sum is agreed upon, and he can collect a reasonable hire if his automobile is used by another without his knowledge or consent. Criminal liability also is attached to the unlawful use of another's automobile.

5. THE SPEED OF AUTOMOBILES along a public road is regulated by law. Some state laws prescribe the maximum rates of speed for business districts, residential districts, and country roads. A municipality has the right to modify the speed laws in accordance with local requirements. Courts of most states hold that it is the duty of a driver on a public highway to have his car under control and to operate it at a reasonable rate of speed, having regard to the traffic and other conditions. He must so operate it as to avoid endangering the life or limb of any person or the safety of anyone's property.

6. THE LAWS OF THE ROAD are intended to prevent collisions and accidents.

a. Vehicles approaching each other from opposite directions are required to keep to the right of the road. If, therefore, two automobiles collide in a street that is wide enough for safe passage, the driver on the left side of the road is responsible for the other driver's injury, provided of course that the other was not himself guilty of negligence.

b. Each driver must pass on his right side of the center of the traveled road. This applies even to roads covered with snow, to side roads, and to roads under construction.

c. It is the duty of every driver to exercise reasonable care in avoiding accidents or injuries to others. This rule applies just as strongly when the driver's car is on the right side of the road.

d. At street intersections it is customary to allow the right of way to the vehicle approaching from the right and, in many states and municipalities, this rule has been embodied in the statutes and ordinances.

e. It is the duty of the driver to keep his car under control at all times.

f. If one willfully or negligently drives a car on a street or road at an unlawful speed, thereby killing another, he may be guilty of homicide.

g. The driver of a car may be charged with negligence if, without warning to others, he suddenly changes the course of his vehicle or backs his car.

7. THE FITNESS OF THE DRIVER—The driver of an automobile should be physically and mentally fit. A man who is subject to fainting spells or epileptic attacks has no right to drive a car upon the public highway. The same rule applies to one with defective eyesight, but it has been held that proper eyeglasses may restore the competency of the driver. No person should ever attempt to drive an automobile while intoxicated, thereby endangering the lives of others.

8. THE CHAUFFEUR'S LIABILITY—As a general rule the owner is liable for the acts of his chauffeur, provided the chauffeur is acting within the scope of the owner's business. However, should the chauffeur use the car without the consent or knowledge of the owner, or should he be using it for his own business and without the owner's consent, the owner is not liable for the driver's acts. The same rule applies when the owner's child uses the parent's car without the parent's knowledge or consent. If the car is run with his knowledge by a member of his family, or for the convenience of other members of the family, the parent may be liable for the negligent acts of the driver. Most states require a chauffeur to take out a license.

9. MINORS—The statutes of most states forbid children

under a certain age to drive automobiles. The ages vary in different states. Thus the owner of a car who allows a child to operate it may be held responsible for accident or injury resulting from the child's negligence.

10. THE CHAUFFEUR'S RIGHTS—A chauffeur may recover damages from his employer for injury received while operating the car, provided that the employer is in some way responsible for the injury. On the other hand, if his injury was due to a defective part, he could not recover from his employer unless it so happened that the employer knew of the defect and the chauffeur did not. If a chauffeur should be injured while riding in a car driven by the owner, the chauffeur could recover for injuries sustained due to the owner's negligence.

11. THE OWNER'S INJURY—If the owner of a car be injured in any way through the wrongful acts or negligence of his chauffeur, the chauffeur may be held liable.

12. GARAGE KEEPER—A garage keeper is bound to exercise reasonable care with reference to vehicles entrusted to him. The owner of a car is not liable to third parties for the negligence of the garage keeper or his employees in the care and operation of his automobile. If a garage keeper or his employee operates an automobile, the garage keeper is liable for any damage done to the car or to third persons. A public garage, while not considered a public nuisance, is subject to public regulations as to location, odors, noise, and fire hazards. A garage keeper is entitled to a reasonable compensation for storage of a car or for repairs that he has been instructed to make. He is not liable for fire damage to the automobile unless the fire is caused by his own negligence or that of his employees. He is liable for theft if he fails to use reasonable precautions to guard against it. See also BAILMENTS.

13. NEW CAR PURCHASE—The law treats a new car much like any other goods—the manufacturer and seller make an implied warranty that the product is safe for its usual uses. See also PRODUCTS LIABILITY.

14. USED AUTOMOBILES—The dealer is required by law to inspect a used automobile and tell the buyer about any flaw that would make it dangerous to operate. However, the seller's responsibility is less than for a new car. The buyer accepts responsibility for any visible defects and, unless otherwise specified in a written contract, he cannot force the dealer to repair mechanical failures. The buyer must beware when purchasing a used automobile.

15. BILL OF SALE—Statutes in most states require that a

bill of sale be given, and the purchaser should be careful to see that the statute is complied with. The bill of sale should be drawn in accordance with the laws of the state where the purchase is made.

The following form will answer the purpose in most of the states:

BILL OF SALE

Know all men by these presents, that I (here insert name and address of party selling the car) in the county of ...., state of .... , in consideration of (here insert amount of money to be paid party selling by party buying) dollars this day to me in hand paid, do hereby grant, sell, transfer and deliver unto the said (here insert name of party buying) the following goods and chattels, to wit: (then insert name of automobile, its model, the engine number and the car number, also the type of car, its color, together with any other information that will help to identify it); to have and to hold said goods and chattels to the said (name of purchaser), his executors, administrators and assigns to their use forever.

I hereby covenant with the said grantee that I am the lawful owner of the said goods and chattels; that they are free and clear from all incumbrances; that I have good right to sell the same and that I will warrant and defend the same against the lawful claims and demands of all persons.

In witness whereof, I, the said (name of party selling) hereunto set my hand and seal the ...... day of ...., 19 ....

Signature of party selling .... (Seal)

16.   THE DRIVER'S RESPONSIBILITIES —The driver of a vehicle involved in a collision has certain responsibilities:
a.   Do not drive away without reporting the facts to the police or nearest police station, or without giving your name, address, and license number to the other party involved. Leaving the scene of an accident may constitute a crime punishable by fine or imprisonment.
b.   Be sure to get the name and address of the other party or, if he drives away, his license number.
c.   Get the names and addresses of all persons who witnessed the accident, or saw the results of it, including all injured persons.
d.   Try to visualize just how it happened, remember your

own position and that of the other party, both before and after the accident, and note carefully the wheel marks on the road or pavement.

e. Be calm and courteous. Do not admit that you are in the wrong or accuse the other party.

f. Do not make immediate settlement or offer to do so, or incur any expense except for necessary medical relief.

Bailment

1. DEFINITIONS—A *bailment* is a delivery of a thing in trust for some special object or purpose with the understanding, expressed or implied, that the person receiving it shall return it when that purpose has been fulfilled. A *bailor* is one who makes a bailment or delivers goods to a *bailee*. A *bailee* is a person who receives goods of another to hold according to the purpose of delivery.

2. BAILOR AND BAILEE—To create this relationship the property must be delivered to the bailee. Thus if A takes his car to a public garage to remain overnight, the garage owner becomes a bailee for hire. The contract of bailment also exists when a man takes a suit of clothes to a tailor shop to be altered, or when a farmer takes a load of oats to a mill to be ground.

3. THE BAILEE'S RESPONSIBILITY—A bailee can limit his liability by agreement, provided the limitation is not in violation of law or public policy and does not excuse him from negligence or fraud on his part. He becomes the custodian of the goods and is generally required to exert reasonable care against accident or loss resulting from the nature of the goods stored. For example, if a truckload of fruit arrives at a cold-storage plant, the owner is not responsible for any loss due to the condition of the fruit when it arrived. On the other hand, if an employee of the storage company negligently allows the goods to spoil, the owner of the fruit can recover from the storage company.

Suppose your bank grants you the privilege of keeping a strongbox in the bank building without paying the normal charges. The bank, of course, is not bound to exercise as much care as a regular safety deposit company, but it is required to take reasonable precaution, that is, as much care as it uses to protect its own property. Suppose a cashier steals the box. Would the bank be liable to you for the loss? If the bank exercised reasonable care, and if the cashier were a long-trusted employee against whom there was no cause for suspicion, the bank would not be held responsible.

4. THE BAILEE'S DUTY—The bailee is usually a keeper

only. However, if he is keeping livestock, he must supply the food necessary to the animals' good condition. Milch cows must be properly milked; and in case of sickness animals must be given proper medical care and attention. In every case the bailee is required to exercise reasonable care for the goods in the bailment.

5. THE BAILOR'S RESPONSIBILITY—The bailor must pay any reasonable charges incurred in the maintenance and preservation of the goods in the bailment. He must also pay for any services rendered pertaining to the purpose of the bailment, such as fees for storing a car or charges for the services of a cleaner or tailor. If the bailor is unwilling or unable to pay such charges the bailee may keep the goods of the bailment as a lien until full payment is made.

Bankruptcy

1. DEFINITION—*Bankruptcy* is a legally declared condition of solvency, that is, of inability to pay one's debts. The property of a bankrupt is divided among his creditors in proportion to their claims, and the bankrupt is absolved of responsibility for past debts. The bankrupt is entitled to certain exemptions; usually he may keep adequate clothing, some furniture, and the tools of his trade. The Bankruptcy Act of 1938, popularly known as the Chandler Act, now contains the law on this subject.

2. EXEMPT CORPORATIONS—Building and loan associations and municipal, railroad, insurance, and banking corporations are exempt from bankruptcy proceedings because other laws govern their insolvency.

3. BANKRUPTS—Bankrupts are of two classes, voluntary and involuntary. *Voluntary bankrupts* are those who are declared bankrupt upon their own petitions. Under the new act, any person or nonexempt corporation owing debts is entitled to the benefits of the act as a voluntary bankrupt. *Involuntary bankrupts* are those who are declared bankrupt on petitions from their creditors. Any nonexempt corporation or any person, except farmers and those earning less than $1,500 a year, owing debts to the amount of $1,000 or over, may be adjudged an involuntary bankrupt.

4. ACTS OF BANKRUPTCY—To have a person declared an involuntary bankrupt his creditors must show that he has committed any of the following acts of bankruptcy:

a. Transferred, concealed, or removed any part of his property with the intent to delay or defraud his creditors.

b. Transferred, while insolvent, any portion of his property to one or more of his creditors with the intent to prefer such creditors over his other creditors.

c. Permitted, while insolvent, any creditor to obtain a lien upon any of his property and not discharged that lien within thirty days.

d. Made a general assignment for the benefit of his creditors, that is, transferred property to his creditors as a group in order to repay his debts.

e. Admitted in writing his inability to pay his debts and his willingness to be adjudged a bankrupt.

5. FILING A VOLUNTARY PETITION—Any eligible person who wishes to declare bankruptcy should file his petition with the clerk of the court in the district where he has had his principal place of business or his domicile for the preceding six months. With the petition he must file (a) a schedule listing the names of his creditors, their residences, the amount due each, and what security each holds, (b) a description of the petitioner's property showing its nature, location, and value, and (c) his claim for any legal exemptions. As soon as these documents are submitted and verified, the petitioner is declared a bankrupt.

6. FILING AN INVOLUNTARY PETITION—If a nonexempt person owing debts to the amount of $1,000 has committed an act of bankruptcy, three or more creditors who have provable claims against such person amounting to $500 or more may file a petition to have him adjudged a bankrupt. If the alleged bankrupt has fewer than twelve creditors, the petition may be filed by one creditor whose claim totals $500 or more. The petition must be duly signed and verified and include the following information and allegations:

a. The name of the alleged bankrupt.

b. That he has had his principal place of business within the judicial district for the preceding six months.

c. That he owes debts to the amount of $1,000 and is not exempt from the laws of bankruptcy.

d. The names and addresses of the petitioning creditors.

e. That they have provable claims against the alleged bankrupt amounting to $500 or more.

f. The nature and amount of petitioners' claims.

g. That within the four months preceding the filing of the petition, the alleged bankrupt committed an act of bankruptcy.

h. A statement as to what acts on his part are alleged to have constituted said act of bankruptcy.

Upon receiving the petition the clerk will issue a subpoena and a copy of the petition to the alleged bankrupt, who has opportunity to file an answer within a certain time. The court may appoint a receiver to take charge of the alleged bankrupt's property if it is necessary to prevent loss. If the alleged bankrupt fails to reply within the time allowed, the court will adjudicate him bankrupt if the petition is in correct form.

7. HEARING IN INVOLUNTARY PROCEEDINGS—If the alleged bankrupt wishes to deny any of the matters set out in the petition, he may do so by filing his sworn answer within the time allowed by law. The matter will then be set down for hearing, and on the day set the petitioners must prove the allegations in their petition or the court will dismiss it. If the allegations are proven, the court will enter the order of adjudication and set a date for the first meeting of the creditors. The bankrupt is then required to file schedules of his creditors, his property, and his exemptions similar to those filed by a voluntary bankrupt.

8. PROCEDURE OUTLINE—After adjudication, the procedure for voluntary and involuntary bankruptcy is the same. The court calls a meeting of the creditors, presided over by a referee. Creditors file proof of their claims and elect a trustee, and the bankrupt is questioned publicly. The trustee takes charge of the estate and calls further meetings as necessary. When his estate has been liquidated and distributed among his creditors, the bankrupt is discharged.

9. STATEMENT OF AFFAIRS—At least five days prior to the first meeting of his creditors, the bankrupt must file a formal statement of his affairs. This information will assist the creditors and the trustee in administering the bankrupt's affairs and in examining the bankrupt.

10. FIRST MEETING OF CREDITORS—The court must schedule the first meeting of the creditors to be held not less than ten nor more than thirty days after adjudication. At that time creditors file proof of their claims against the bankrupt and appoint a trustee to act as their representative in taking charge of the bankrupt's estate and converting his assets to cash. In addition, the creditors may appoint a committee of three or more of their number to consult with and advise the trustee in the administration of the estate. The referee or trustee must examine the bankrupt at this meeting.

11. FUNCTION OF THE REFEREE—The referee is the officer of the court who is in charge of a bankruptcy proceeding. He presides at all meetings of the creditors, holds evidence and records, and furnishes information to interested parties. He must verify and accept each claim before the creditor can vote at meetings; he is empowered to hold hearings and pass judgment on contested issues. He supervises the examination of the bankrupt, but usually

delegates the actual questioning to the trustee. He audits the accounts of the trustee and grants final discharge to the bankrupt.

12. RESPONSIBILITY OF THE TRUSTEE—The trustee must liquidate the bankrupt's estate, that is, convert his property into cash, and distribute the proceeds among the creditors. He usually examines the bankrupt publicly in order to determine that the bankrupt has not fraudulently concealed any property or given unlawful preference to any creditor. He must recover any property wrongfully removed from the estate, sell all property for the best price available, and bring necessary legal actions on behalf of the estate. He may make contracts as agent for the estate. He is accountable to the creditors and to the referee.

13. PROOF OF CLAIMS—In order to share in any dividends that may be paid to creditors out of the property of the bankrupt, a creditor must file his claim in court within six months after the first meeting of creditors, prove his claim, and have it allowed by the court. Only claims provable in law or equity are provable in bankruptcy; contingent claims are not provable. The law requires that a written proof of claim signed by the creditor be filed setting forth (a) the claim, (b) the consideration therefor, (c) what securities are held against it, (d) what payments have been made on the debt, and (e) that the claim is justly owing from the bankrupt to the creditor. Any written instrument supporting the claim should be filed with the proof of claim. Properly presented claims are allowed unless objected to by parties in interest or by the court. If objected to, they are set down for hearing before the referee.

14. VOTING AT MEETINGS—Matters submitted to creditors at their meetings are passed upon by vote of a majority in number of all proven creditors who are present, which number must also represent a majority in amount of all proven debts of the bankrupt. Relatives of the bankrupt or, when the bankrupt is a corporation, its stockholders, officers, and directors, are not allowed to vote. Creditors holding claims that are secured or have priority are not entitled to vote on the strength of such claims. Such claims are not counted in computing either the number of creditors or the amount of their claims, except in cases where the amounts of such claims exceed the values of such securities and priorities, and then only for such excess. Claims of $50 or less are not counted in computing the number of creditors voting or present at meetings, but shall be counted in computing the amount.

15. SUBSEQUENT MEETINGS—The trustee may call a meeting of the creditors whenever he deems it necessary. In addition, the law provides that the court shall call a meeting of creditors whenever one-fourth or more in number of those who have proven their claims shall file a written request for a meeting. Whenever the affairs of the bankrupt's estate are ready to be closed, the court orders a final meeting of creditors. A case in which there are no assets may be closed without such final meeting.

16. LEGAL EXEMPTIONS—The kinds of property that cannot be taken from a bankrupt are established by the laws of the various states. Generally, the bankrupt cannot be reduced to destitution, that is, left without adequate clothing and shelter, nor be deprived of the tools of his trade. See EX-EMPTIONS.

17. PRIORITY OF CLAIMS—Before distributing any proceeds of the estate among the creditors, the trustee must meet certain obligations. Property and funds held in trust by the bankrupt must be returned to the rightful owners, and certain debts and expenses must be paid in the following priority:

a. Costs incurred in maintaining and administering the estate, such as storage fees, fees for filing petitions, and fees for referee, trustee, and lawyers.
b. Wages due employees of the bankrupt up to $600 per employee.
c. All taxes, whether federal, state, or local.
d. Certain kinds of debts granted priority by state or federal law.

18. DISCHARGE OF THE BANKRUPT—The discharge in bankruptcy is the final ruling of the court releasing the bankrupt from all past debts voidable through bankruptcy. A bankrupt cannot be discharged if he has acted fraudulently to obtain credit while insolvent, if he has attempted to defraud his creditors or to conceal material information during bankruptcy proceedings, or if he has been discharged from bankruptcy during the past six years. A bankrupt corporation may file an application for discharge within six months after its adjudication. A bankrupt individual need not file such application, for his adjudication operates as an application for discharge. After the bankrupt individual has been examined, the court fixes a time for the filing of objections to the bankrupt's discharge and gives notice to all parties in interest. If no objection is filed within the fixed time, the court discharges the bankrupt. A discharge in bankruptcy releases the bankrupt from all of his provable debts except the following:

a. Taxes.

b. Liabilities for obtaining money by false pretenses, for willful and malicious injuries to the person or property of another, for alimony or support of wife or child, for seduction, or for adultery.

c. Debts not scheduled in time for proof and allowance, unless the creditor had notice or actual knowledge of the proceedings in bankruptcy.

d. Liabilities created by the bankrupt's fraud or embezzlement while acting as an officer or in any fiduciary capacity.

e. Wages due to employees of the bankrupt.

f. Debts for moneys deposited with the bankrupt by his employee as security for the faithful performance of the terms of a contract of employment.

19. COMPOSITION—After a bankrupt has filed the schedule of his property and list of his creditors and has been examined in open court or at a meeting of creditors, he may offer terms of *composition*. That is, he offers to make immediate payment of a certain proportion of each general claim provided the creditor will release him from the balance. The bankrupt must still pay the whole amount owing on any priority claims. This is, of course, precisely what happens by operation of law if the bankruptcy proceeding is carried to a conclusion, but a composition is often more desirable because it can be carried out at once, thus dispensing with a good many of the costs of longer proceedings and preserving the estate in cases where the property is of a nature that will deteriorate or accumulate expense during a delay. Then, too, if the composition is confirmed by the court the debtor is spared some of the ignominy of having gone through bankruptcy and received a discharge. Before being filed in court, the composition must have been accepted in writing by a majority in number of all creditors whose claims have been allowed, which number must also represent a majority in amount of such claims. When the application for confirmation of the composition is filed in court, the money necessary to carry the composition into effect, together with that necessary to pay all debts that have priority and to pay the costs of the proceedings that have already taken place, must be deposited in a place designated by the judge. If the judge is then satisfied at a hearing that the composition is for the best interests of the creditors and is offered by the bankrupt in good faith, he will confirm it and dismiss the case after each creditor has received his share of the money set aside by the bankrupt as a consideration for the composition. The confirmation of a composition

has the same effect as a discharge in that it releases all debts of the bankrupt that would be released by a discharge in regular form.

Bonds

1. DEFINITIONS—A *bond* is a certificate of obligation, usually an evidence of debt. It is a form of contract that is almost infinite in variety. The parties to the bond are the *obligor* and the *obligee,* the former being the one who makes the promise and the latter the person to whom the promise is made.

2. A SIMPLE BOND is an instrument promising payment of money at a certain time, and generally bears interest at the rate specified in the bond. Nearly all corporate and municipal bonds are of this character and contain no condition except for the payment of the amount of the bond at a certain time and place with a certain specified rate of interest. Frequently interest coupons are attached to the original bond, providing for the payment of the several installments of interest as they come due.

The following is the form commonly in use for such bonds:

UNITED STATES OF AMERICA.
JEFFERSON CITY, STATE OF MISSOURI.
RENEWAL SCHOOL BOND.
INTEREST 6 PER CENT, PAYABLE SEMI-ANNUALLY.

The Board of Education of the City of Jefferson, County of Cole, and State of Missouri, being legally organized under and pursuant to an act of the General Assembly of the State of Missouri entitled "An act to revise and amend the Laws in relation to Public Schools in Cities, Towns and Villages," approved April 26th, 19 . . ., for value received promise to pay to the bearer ten years after the date hereof One Thousand Dollars ($1,000) at the St. Louis National Bank, in the City of St. Louis, Missouri, together with interest thereon at the rate of six per centum per annum from the date hereof, which interest shall be payable semi-annually at said St. Louis National Bank in the City of St. Louis, Missouri, on the surrender of the proper interest coupons hereto attached. This bond shall be redeemable at the pleasure of the said Board of Education of the City of Jefferson at any time after the expiration of five years from the date hereof, and is issued under and pursuant to an act of the General Assembly of the State of Missouri, entitled "An Act to Authorize Boards of Education to Issue Renewal Funding School Bonds," to be sold or exchanged for the purpose of meeting and paying matured or maturing bonded indebtedness of school districts and for levying special tax to pay the bonded indebtedness of school districts, approved April 11th, 19 . . . .

In Testimony Whereof: the said Board of Education has caused this bond to be signed by the President, countersigned by the Secretary, authenticated by the seal of said Board of Education and attested by the Clerk of the County Court of said County of Cole, with the seal of said Court affixed this First day of July, 19 . . . .

> JOHN JONES, President
> WM. SMITH, Secretary
> GEO. SMILEY, Clerk County
> Court

3. SURETY BONDS—*Surety bonds* are obligations to pay a certain sum of money on condition that if the bonded person—the *obligor*—faithfully performs his duties, the obligation is void. This type of bond is in common use for a variety of purposes. All state, county, town, and city officers who handle public funds must give bond to assure the honest and proper performance of their official duties.

The following form of a bond of city treasurer can be used with a few slight changes for almost any office:

> Know all men by these presents, That we, John Jones, Henry Smith, and Charles Marshall of the City of Naperville, County of Du Page, and State of Illinois, are held and firmly bound unto the City of Naperville in the penal sum of Twenty Thousand Dollars ($20,-000), for the payment of which, well and truly to be made, we bind ourselves, our heirs, executors, and administrators jointly and firmly by these presents.

> Witness our hands and seals this 14th day of July, 19 . . . .

> The condition of the above obligation is such that whereas the said John Jones has been duly elected to the office of City Treasurer of the City of Naperville; Now if the said John Jones shall faithfully perform all the duties of said office and shall account for and pay over all moneys that may come into his hands as such Treasurer, according to law and the ordinances of said

City and the order and direction of the City Council of said City, then this obligation is to be void, otherwise to remain in full force and effect.

JOHN JONES	(Seal)
HENRY SMITH	(Seal)
CHARLES MARSHALL	(Seal)

4. BUSINESS—Officers of corporations are often required to give surety bonds for the faithful performance of their duties. The following form can be used for nearly all such bonds:

Know all men by these presents, That we, James Lord, John Williams, and Charles Smith, are held and firmly bound unto the Naperville Manufacturing Company, a corporation duly organized under the laws of the State of Illinois, in the penal sum of Ten Thousand Dollars ($10,000), good and lawful money of the United States, for the payment of which, well and truly to be made to said corporation or its assigns, we bind ourselves jointly and severally.

Witness our hands and seals this 14th day of July, 19 . . . .

The condition of the above obligation is such that whereas the said James Lord has been elected President of the Naperville Manufacturing Company; Now Therefore, if the said James Lord shall well and truly perform the duties of his said office and shall account for and pay over all moneys that shall come into his hands as such President, and do all required of him by the bylaws of said corporation now in force or hereafter enacted, and obey all orders given him by the board of directors of said corporation, then this obligation shall be void, otherwise to remain in full force and effect.

JAMES LORD	(Seal)
JOHN WILLIAMS	(Seal)
CHARLES SMITH	(Seal)

5. INDEMNIFYING BONDS—Bonds are also frequently given to indemnify persons who incur liability for another in many other walks of life. The following form may be used:

Know all men by these presents, That William Marsh, Principal, and John Henry, Surety, are held and firmly bound unto John Jones in the penal sum of One Hundred Dollars ($100), lawful money of the United States, for the payment of which, well and truly to be made, we bind ourselves, our heirs, executors, and administrators, jointly, severally and firmly by these presents.

Witness our hands and seals this 1st day of June, A.D. 19 . . . . .

The condition of the above obligation is such that whereas the said John Jones has been surety for the above William Marsh on his note for One Thousand Dollars ($1,000) payable to the order of Charles William, due in one year from the date hereof, with in- ·terest at the rate of 6 per cent per annum.

Now, Therefore, if the said William Marsh shall well and truly pay the said note with all interest thereon when the same comes due and shall from time to time and at all times hereafter save, keep harmless and indemnify the said John Jones of and from all actions, suits, costs, charges, damages, and expenses whatsoever, including attorney's fees, which shall or may at any time hereafter happen or come to him for any reason, by reason of his becoming surety on said note, then this obligation is to be void, otherwise to remain in full force and effect.

WILLIAM MARSH	(Seal)
JOHN HENRY	(Seal)

6. EXECUTOR'S BOND—Executors, administrators, guardians, and conservators are required to enter into bonds to be approved by the proper court before they are allowed to enter upon their duties as such. The forms for such bonds, however, vary in the different states.

Broker

1. DEFINITIONS—A *broker* is a middleman or negotiator between parties. He conducts transactions in his specialized field, but he does not have custody of the property. The person who employs a broker is called the *principal*. *Brokerage* is the fee charged by a broker for transacting business.

2. WHY BROKERS ARE EMPLOYED—Brokers are often employed to transact business or to negotiate bargains between different individuals. By specializing in a single line or a limited number of lines of business, they acquire a

knowledge and skill that an average merchant does not possess. It is often advantageous for large firms to employ brokers to buy their raw materials. Brokers may also specialize in real estate, insurance, or securities. The business of brokerage is regulated largely by the customs of the particular trade.

3. A BROKER'S LIABILITY — A broker usually has no special property in the goods he sells. If he does not disclose the principal's name he is liable to the same extent as other agents. (See AGENCY: AGENTS' RESPONSIBILITY.) He must serve faithfully and cannot act for both parties in the same transaction without the consent and knowledge of both. Neither can he delegate his powers without the principal's assent. He is bound to obey the express instructions of his principal, and to keep accurate accounts of his transactions.

4. A BROKER'S COMPENSATION — Usually a broker's compensation is a commission or percentage of the value of the thing sold or exchanged. If the amount of the compensation is not fixed, the custom of the trade rules. A broker is entitled to a reasonable compensation for his services.

5. A REAL ESTATE BROKER must act for his principal alone. He is employed to negotiate sales and exchanges of land, and often has such additional duties as renting real estate, collecting rent, and procuring loans. To gain his commission on the sale he must produce a customer who is ready, able, and willing to accept and live up to the terms of the sale. A property owner cannot avoid paying the commission or brokerage by selling the property himself, or at a lower price than he listed with the broker.

6. PAWNBROKERS — The business of a pawnbroker, the rate of interest he may charge, and the sale of pawned goods are usually regulated by law. A license is usually required and the business is always subject to regulation and control. Suppose A takes a watch to a pawnbroker who advances him $20. A, or his assignee, or the purchaser of the pawn ticket, may redeem it within the fixed time, or even beyond that time if the pawnbroker has not exercised his right to sell the watch. A, the pawner, has the right to assign or sell his interest in the watch. If A fails to redeem the watch, the pawnbroker can usually hold him for any deficiency after the watch is sold.

Carriers

1. DEFINITIONS — A *carrier* is a person or company that undertakes, or whose business it is, to carry persons or merchandise for hire. Carriers are of two kinds, private and common. A *private carrier* is one who carries only occa-

sionally, and not as a public business. Such a carrier need not serve all who wish to employ him, but is liable for negligence in transporting the goods he accepts. A *common carrier* is one whose regular business it is to carry goods or passengers from place to place for all persons who elect to employ and pay him.

2. EXAMPLES—A private carrier is usually an individual who, without being engaged in such business as a public employment, carries merchandise from one point to another for a consideration. He is bound to exercise such care of the property as a man of ordinary intelligence would his own property. Common carriers hold themselves out to carry goods or passengers from one place to another, for all persons who offer to employ them. Examples of common carriers are railroad companies, steamship companies, street-car companies, taxicab companies, truckmen, and express companies.

3. BILL OF LADING—A *bill of lading* is the receipt given by the common carrier to the owner of the goods desiring to have the same shipped, and should contain a description of (a) the quantity, (b) the marks on the merchandise, (c) the names of the shipper or the person sending the goods, the consignee, and the person to whom the goods are shipped, (d) the place of departure and place of discharge of the goods, (e) the price of freight, and (f) the weight of the separate packages and the number of the car in which the same were shipped.

4. RESPONSIBILITY—Common carriers are generally responsible for all loss and damage caused by transportation from whatever cause, except the act of God or of the public enemy, and they are bound to carry all goods that are offered them, provided such goods come within the class of articles they hold themselves out to carry. The carrier is not responsible for losses occurring from natural causes, such as frosts, fermentation, or natural decay of perishable articles, or the necessary and natural wear in the course of transportation, provided the carrier exercises all reasonable care to keep the loss or deterioration as minimal as practical. The carrier is liable for any and all loss occasioned by accidental fire.

5. PERISHABLE GOODS—Carriers are not responsible for loss to fruits that decay in their possession through no fault of theirs or for goods shipped in defective boxes, such as glassware and other easily broken articles that are not properly packed. Goods must be properly packed in order to make the carrier responsible.

6. BAGGAGE—In the transportation of the baggage of passengers the liability of the carrier for loss to the same is

the same as in the case of transportation of goods for hire, and in case of loss the carrier must make it good.

7. WHEN LIABILITY BEGINS AND ENDS—The responsibility of the common carrier begins upon the delivery of the goods for immediate transportation. A delivery at the usual place of receiving freight or to the employee of the company in the usual course of business is sufficient. The responsibility of the carrier as such terminates after the arrival of the goods at their destination and sufficient time has elapsed thereafter for the owner to have received them during business hours. After the expiration of such time the responsibility of the carrier is simply that of a warehouseman and he is required only to keep the goods with ordinary care.

8. LIMITATION OF LIABILITY—A carrier can limit his liability by contract, unless forbidden by statute. Thus a statement limiting the amount of a carrier's liability may be put on a bill of lading given as a receipt for a freight or express shipment, or on a receipt for a freight or express shipment, or on a receipt given a passenger for his baggage. Such statement is considered binding by the courts and relieves the carrier of additional liability. The general rule is that a carrier may relieve himself from all liability except for loss or damage caused by his own negligence.

9. THE PASSENGER'S RIGHTS—The law requires common carriers to carry all passengers who pay the required fare and who are in a sufficiently intelligent condition to travel. The carrier must exercise great care in transporting passengers and is liable for injury due to the carrier's negligence. If the passenger was himself negligent and contributed to his own injury, he cannot as a rule hold the carrier liable.

10. EQUAL LIABILITY—Railroad companies and other carriers who allow express companies to carry parcels and packages on their cars or other vehicles are as liable as the common carriers for all damages that occur, without regard to the contract between them and such express company.

11. DIFFERENT LINES—Where goods are accepted for shipment to points beyond the line of the carrier to whom they are first delivered, such carrier is responsible for the delivery of the goods at their destination. The law now provides that under such circumstances the carrier shall be liable for any loss or injury occurring during the shipment, whether on its own line or on that of the connecting carrier.

12. DEMURRAGE is the sum charged by transportation companies for goods not removed from their cars within the time fixed by the rules of the companies. The rules of a large number of railroad companies require that the cars be unloaded within twenty-four hours after the train's arrival at the destination. A fixed rate of demurrage for each twen-

ty-four hours of delay after the expiration of the usual time for unloading is imposed on the persons to whom goods are shipped.

13. THE CARRIER'S RIGHTS—The carrier is entitled to a reasonable compensation for his services, and may demand payment in advance. The shipper is liable for freight, unless the carrier agrees to look exclusively to some other party. After delivery the carrier may recover the amount of freight from the consignee. But freight may be collected only for the goods actually delivered, unless the delivery be prevented by the owner or unless it be agreed that freight shall be payable regardless of losses by the way. The carrier also has a lien on the goods for his freight and advances on such goods, and may refuse to deliver until such charges be paid. This lien has priority over the owner's right of stoppage in transit and the claims of the general creditors of the owner or consignee. A carrier by water also has a lien for salvage and for customs duties advanced on imported goods.

14. COMMUNICATIONS—Telegraph and telephone companies are not common carriers and may therefore establish their own regulations for the transmission of messages. Like common carriers, however, they are required to serve all who apply and offer to pay the charges, and are liable for damages when messages are not sent promptly and accurately. They come within the classification of public service corporations, and are subject to legislative regulation and control as to kind of service to be rendered and rates for such service.

Chattel Mortgage

1. DEFINITIONS—A *chattel mortgage* is an instrument by which the owner conveys conditional title to personal property to secure the payment of a debt or the performance of a contract or other obligation. It is a pledge that the debt will be paid. Any personal property that may be sold may be mortgaged, such as automobiles, livestock, machinery, farm implements, life-insurance policies, corporation stock, and crops. The *mortgagor* is the person who conveys the property. The *mortgagee* is the person to whom the transfer is made.

2. FORM OF MORTGAGE—The usual form of a chattel mortgage is a bill of sale with the *conditional clause* stating the terms of the loan, and that on the mortgagor's failure to pay, the mortgagee may take possession of the property. Any person competent to make a contract, or his agent, may make a chattel mortgage. Partners or joint tenants may mortgage jointly on their individual interests. A corporation

may also mortgage its personal property.

Chattel mortgages are usually given to secure notes in the same way in which real estate mortgages are given to secure notes. Greater strictness, however, is required in the acknowledgment, docketing, and recording of chattel mortgages than in the case of real estate mortgages. A chattel mortgage must be acknowledged before a justice of the peace or some other person authorized by law to take acknowledgments.

3. DESCRIBING THE PROPERTY—The property mortgaged must be described clearly enough to enable third persons to identify it, but this is determined largely by the nature of the chattels. "All" articles in a stated place is generally a valid description.

4. FORECLOSURE—When the mortgagor fails to pay his debt, the right of the mortgagee to proceed in taking the property is regulated by law. In most chattel mortgages a clause is included permitting the mortgagee to seize and sell the property should the mortgagor fail to make payment.

5. GENERAL PRINCIPLES—A chattel mortgage remains in effect as between the parties themselves until it is released or becomes barred by what is known as the statute of limitations. However, in order to preserve the mortgage's validity against creditors of the mortgagor and subsequent purchasers of the mortgaged property, it must be refiled or renewed periodically. The periods vary in different states but are generally from one to three years. To sell property covered by a chattel mortgage for a valuable consideration without notifying the purchaser of the existence of the mortgage is a criminal offense. Statutes in a few states provide that notes secured by chattel mortgages must show on their faces that they are secured by chattel mortgages, or they are absolutely void. In other states, chattel mortgages on household goods must be signed by both the mortgagor and his wife. See also MORTGAGE; SECURED TRANSACTIONS.

6. FORMS—The following forms are often used for the various documents relating to chattel mortgages.

CHATTEL MORTGAGE WITH POWER OF SALE

Know all men by these presents, that I, A.B., in consideration of the sum of $........ paid by C.D., have bargained and sold, and by these presents do hereby sell and convey to said C.D., the following goods and chattels, to wit: (describe the articles mortgaged, or refer to them as the goods and chattels mentioned in the schedule hereto annexed), and which are now in my possession.

Whereas, the said A.B. is justly indebted to C.D., in the sum of $............, payable on the ....day of ...., 19......, with interest at six per cent from the ....day of ...., 19......, (upon a promissory note of even date herewith, or for goods sold and delivered).

Now the condition of the above obligation is such that if the said A.B. shall well and truly pay the said C.D. said sum of money and interest when the same shall become due, then this conveyance shall be void, otherwise to remain in full force and effect. It is also agreed that said A.B. may retain possession of the said mortgaged property until said debt becomes due. But if default be made in the payment of said sum or any part thereof, the said C.D. and his assigns are hereby authorized to sell said goods and chattels, or so much thereof as will be necessary to satisfy the amount then due, together with the cost and expenses incurred by reason of said default.

(Signed)   A.B.
In the presence of E.F.

MORTGAGE ON GOODS AND CHATTELS

Know all men by these presents, that A.B., residing at ...., of the first part, for securing the payment of the ...., hereinafter mentioned, and in consideration of the sum of One Dollar ($1), to ..... in hand paid, at or before the execution and delivery of these presents, by C.D., of the second part, the receipt whereof is hereby acknowledged, has (have) granted, bargained, sold, and assigned, and by these presents does (do) grant, bargain, sell, and assign unto the said party (parties) of the second part, all .... now remaining and being ....

To have and to hold, all and singular, the goods and chattels above bargained and sold, or intended so to be, unto the said party (parties) of the second part, ... executors, administrators, and assigns forever. And the said party (parties) of the first part, for .... heirs, executors, and administrators, all and singular, the said goods and chattels above bargained and sold unto the said party (parties) of the second part, ... executors, administrators, and assigns, against the said party (parties) of the first part, and against all and every person or persons whomsoever shall and will warrant, and by these presents forever defend.

Upon condition, that if the said party (parties) of the first part shall and does (do) well and truly pay, or cause to be paid, unto the said party (parties) of the second part, ... executors, administrators, or assigns, the sum of ...., then these presents and everything herein contained shall cease and be void. And the said party (parties) of the first part, for .... executors, administrators, and assigns, does (do) covenant and agree to and with the said party (parties) of the second part, ... executors, administrators, and assigns, to make punctual payment of the money hereby secured .... And in case default shall be made in payment of the said sum above mentioned, or in case the said party (parties) of the second part shall sooner choose to demand the said goods and chattels, it shall and may be lawful for, and the said party (parties) of the first part does (do) hereby authorize and empower the said party (parties) of the second part, ... executors, administrators, and assigns, with the aid and assistance of any person or persons, to enter and come into and upon the dwelling house and premises of the said party (parties) of the first part, and in such other place or places as the said goods and chattels are or may be held or placed, and take and carry away the said goods and chattels to sell and dispose of the same for the best price he (they) can obtain, at either public or private sale, and out of the money to retain and pay the said sum above mentioned, with the interest and all expenses and charges thereon, rendering the overplus (if any) unto the said party (parties) of the first part, ... executors, administrators, and assigns. And until default be made in the payment of the aforesaid sum of money, the said party (parties) of the first part to remain and continue in quiet and peaceable possession of the said goods and chattels, and the full and free enjoyment of the same, unless the said party (parties) of the second part, ... executors, administrators, or assigns, shall sooner choose to demand the same; and until such demand be made, the possession of the said party (parties) of the first part shall be deemed the possession of an agent or servant, for the sole benefit and advantage of his principal, the said party (parties) of the second part.

In witness whereof, the said party (parties) of the first part, has (have) hereunto set .... hand(s) and seal(s) this .... day of ...., 19.......

Sealed and delivered in the presence of ......,
County of ....ss.:

On this .... day of............, 19........,
before me came ...., to me known to be the
person(s) described in and who executed the foregoing
instrument, and .... acknowledged that he
(they) executed the same.

NOTICE OF SALE UNDER CHATTEL MORTGAGE

Notice is hereby given that by virtue of a chattel
mortgage, dated on the .... day of ....,
19 ......, and duly filed in the office of the county
clerk of .... county, ..., on the .... day
of ...., 19 ....., in book ......, of ....
on page ...., and executed by A. B. to C. D. to
secure the payment of the sum of $ ...., and
upon which there is now due the sum of
$.............. Default having been made in the pay-
ment of said sum, and no suit or other proceeding at
law having been instituted to recover said debt or any
part thereof, therefore, I will sell the property therein
described, viz: (here describe the articles substantially
as in the mortgage) at public auction to the highest
bidder, for cash, at ...., in the (city, town, or
precinct) of ...., in ....
county, on the .... day of ...., at one
o'clock P.M. of said date.

C.D.
Mortagee

Dated ...., 19 ......

ASSIGNMENT OF MORTGAGE

This instrument, made this .... day of ....,
19 ....., between ...., of the first part, and
............., of the second part, witnesseth: That the
party (parties) of the first part, for a good and valuable
consideration, to .... in hand paid by the party
(parties) of the second part, has (have) sold, assigned,
transferred, and conveyed, and does (do) hereby sell,
assign, transfer, and convey to the party (parties) of
the second part, a certain mortgage bearing date the
.... day of ......, 19 ...., made by ....,
recorded in the clerk's office of .... county in
book .... of mortgages, at page ....., on the ....

day of ...., 19 ...., at .... o'clock ..... m.,
together with the bond accompanying said mortgage,
and therein referred to, and all sums of money due
and to grow due thereon. And the party (parties) of the
first part hereby covenant that there is ....
due on the said bond and mortgage the sum of
....

In witness whereof, the party (parties) of the first
part has (have) hereunto set .... hand(s) and
seal(s) the day and year first above written.

Citizenship

1. DEFINITION — A *citizen* is a member of a state or nation
who enjoys political rights and is entitled to public protection. Citizenship, therefore, carries with it the duty of
allegiance to the government and the right of protection by
it.

2. GENERAL PRINCIPLES — A citizen residing in any of the
several states owes an allegiance both to the United States
and to the state, and may demand protection from each
government. A citizen residing in the District of Columbia is
a citizen of the United States only. A citizen's ordinary
rights are protected by the state government.

All persons born or naturalized in the United States and
subject to its jurisdiction or persons born abroad of American parents are citizens of the United States. Formerly a
woman took the citizenship of her husband upon marriage.
Now marriage does not affect the American citizenship of
the wife unless she chooses to renounce it. Neither does
naturalization of the husband operate to confer citizenship
upon the wife.

3. NATURALIZATION — In order to be naturalized, an alien
must follow the forms prescribed by law. His entry into the
country must have been lawful, and he must furnish a certificate showing the time, place, and manner of his arrival.

He must declare on oath, before the clerk of an authorized
court in the district in which he resides, his intention of
becoming a citizen of the United States and of residing here
permanently, and he must renounce all allegiance to any
foreign power. Not less than two nor more than seven years
after he has made such declaration of intention, he must file
his petition for admission to citizenship. He must declare on
oath in open court that he will support and defend the Constitution of the United States, and he must renounce
allegiance to any foreign power. The law also requires that
no alien shall be admitted to citizenship unless immediately

preceding the date of his petition he has resided continuously within the United States for at least five years, and within the county where he resided when he filed his petition for at least six months. Naturalization of the parent confers citizenship on his minor children if they reside in the United States at the time or subsequently begin to reside here permanently.

4. ALIENS' RIGHTS—Aliens have the right to hold and transfer title to real estate. At common law they are entitled to purchase, own, and sell personal property, to engage in business, and to make contracts or wills. In return they must obey the laws of the land in which they reside.

Contracts

1. DEFINITIONS—A *contract* is a mutual agreement between two or more competent parties for a valuable consideration to do or not to do a particular thing. A *simple contract* may or may not be in writing and requires no seal. A *specialty* is a contract in writing that does require a seal to the signatures. An *executed contract* is completed; an *executory contract* is one still to be executed or completed. An *express contract* is a contract actually made between two or more parties; an *implied contract* is one in which some of the provisions or the entire agreement must be implied from previous agreements, from existing customs, or from the acts of the parties.

2. REQUIREMENTS—A contract must have
a. Two or more competent parties.
b. Legal subject matter.
c. Consideration.
d. Assent of the parties.
There cannot be a contract when any of these are wanting.

3. THE FORM OF THE CONTRACT—In many written contracts the parties are referred to as "party of the first part," or "party of the second part," according to the order in which their names first appear. It does not matter which name is written first. A contract contains certain information in the following order:
a. A written contract begins with a statement of the date, the names of the parties, and their places of residence. Then appears a statement of the consideration, followed by a full statement of all that the first party agrees to do, and all that the second party agrees to do.
b. Next appears a statement of the penalties or forfeitures in case either party does not faithfully and fully perform, or offer to perform, his part of the agreement.

c. The contract ends with the signatures of the parties and their seals and the signatures of witnesses. A seal is simply the mark of a pen around the word "seal," written after the signature, or the word "seal" in parentheses printed or typewritten on the form. Many states no longer require this formality.

4. OTHER FACTORS—Competent lawyers should be employed in the drafting of a contract. Errors in grammar or spelling do not affect the legality of the agreement. If the language should be obscure on certain points, the court will try to determine the intent of the parties when they entered into the agreement, providing the intent can be gathered from the terms of the instrument itself. It is of the utmost importance that the terms of the contract be specifically and explicitly stated.

5. THE VITAL PART OF A CONTRACT: CONSIDERATION—A *consideration* is the thing that induces a party to make a contract. It is the substantial cause or reason inducing the parties to enter into an agreement. A *valuable consideration* is one that is equal to money or may be translated into monetary terms. It is sometimes defined as "money or its equivalent." The law does not require that the consideration should be a good or bad bargain. As long as something is done or suffered by either party, always providing it is not illegal, the consideration is good. The smallest consideration is sufficient to make it legal. The value of the consideration is generally unimportant. All considerations that are immoral are consequently illegal, and contracts based upon them are generally void.

6. THE LAW GOVERNING CONTRACTS—Several basic principles of law apply to all contracts.

a. An intentional alteration in a material part of a contract, made by one party without the consent of the other, discharges the other party from his obligations under the contract.

b. A contract made by a minor is not binding upon him, yet he can hold the other party to all the conditions of the contract.

c. A fraudulent contract may be binding on the party guilty of fraud, although not laying any obligation on the part of the party acting in good faith.

d. A contract for the sale or purchase of personal property over a certain amount—ranging from $30 to $500 in the different states—must be in writing.

e. A contract that cannot be performed within a year must be in writing.

f. If no time of payment is stated in the contract, payment

must be made on the delivery of the goods.

g. A contract totally restraining the exercise of a man's trade or profession is void, but one restraining him in any particular place is not void.

h. An offer or proposal that includes the essential parts of a contract becomes a contract as soon as accepted. Generally the acceptance must be at the time of receiving the offer. The offer may be withdrawn at any time before it has been accepted. Offers may be made and accepted within a reasonable time by word of mouth, telephone, telegraph, or mail.

i. A contract required by law to be in writing cannot be changed by verbal agreement.

j. A contract cannot be rescinded except by consent of both parties unless one party has given the other legal grounds to rescind, such as default or fraud.

k. A contract binding in the place where it is made is binding everywhere, but courts of one state will not enforce contracts made in another state where to do so would be in violation of the statutes or public policy of their own state.

l. Each party to an agreement or contract should retain a signed copy.

m. While signatures or contracts written with a pencil are valid in law, it is always safer to write them in ink.

7. UNLAWFUL CONTRACTS—Some kinds of contracts are unlawful or unenforceable by their very nature.

a. A contract to commit a breach of peace.

b. An agreement for immoral purposes.

c. An agreement procured by threats, violence, or fraud.

d. Wagers or bets cannot be collected by law.

e. Interest at rates higher than the maximum rate fixed by law cannot be collected.

f. A contract with an intoxicated person, lunatic, or minor cannot be enforced by the other party.

g. A contract in violation of a statute in the state in which it is made.

h. An agreement to prevent competition on a sale under an execution.

i. An agreement to prohibit the carrying on of a trade throughout the state.

j. Where consent to an agreement is given by mistake and the other party knows of the mistake, such agreement cannot be enforced.

k. The right to vote or hold a public office cannot be sold by contract.

l. A contract without a consideration, such as a promise to make a gift, cannot be enforced.

m. Two or more persons cannot intentionally make a contract to willfully injure a third person.

n. Contracts for concealing felony, for violating public trust, for bribery, or for extortion are prohibited.

o. Useless things, such as agreeing not to go out of the house for a month, cannot become the subject of a contract.

p. A verbal release without payment satisfaction for the debt is not good. Release must be under seal, unless made for some new consideration.

q. If two parts of a contract are in direct conflict with each other, the former part holds good in preference to the latter.

r. Contracts in which there is misrepresentation or concealment of material facts cannot be enforced by the party guilty of such misrepresentation or concealment.

s. If a thing contracted for is not in existence at the time of making the contract, as in a case where parties contract for the purchase and sale of a horse without knowing that the horse is dead at the time, the contract is not valid.

t. If a person agrees to serve as a laborer or clerk, he cannot be compelled to fulfill his agreement; damages, however, can be recovered for a failure to perform.

u. An agreement with a thief to drop a criminal prosecution in consideration of his bringing back the goods and paying all damages is not good and will be no bar to a future prosecution.

v. Guardians, trustees, executors, administrators, or attorneys cannot take advantage of those for whom they act by becoming parties to contracts in which the persons for whom they are acting are interested.

8. QUASI CONTRACTS—A *quasi contract* may be defined as a contract implied in law, or in the nature of a contract. It is a legal obligation resulting from some direct or indirect benefit accruing to one party from the other. Even without any express agreement on the part of the first party, the law compels him to pay. For example

a. One who has reason to believe that payment for goods tendered is expected must not accept them unless he intends to pay for them. If he accepts the goods, he can be compelled to pay for them.

b. A man employed under the promise of good wages or division of profits is entitled to fair treatment, even though such an arrangement is no contract at all.

c. Money paid on an illegal contract, or on one which is void because of nonexistence of the property, may be recovered.

d.   If an express company delivers valuable goods to the wrong party, the company can recover from the person who wrongfully accepted them.

e.   If, on account of a mistake, a man pays his grocery bill twice for the same period, he can recover.

f.   Action to recover can be brought against a man who sells property that is not his own, or that proves to be worthless.

g.   Liability is imposed regardless of consent, as distinguished from a contract implied in fact, which is an actual contract, and based on presumed intent or consent. All these questions hinge on the presence or absence of consideration in the agreement.

9.   STATUTE OF FRAUDS—In every state there is a statute called the *statute of frauds,* which provides that certain contracts must be in writing to bind the parties. Thus

a.   Agreements for the sale of real estate are unenforceable unless they are in writing.

b.   A contract for the sale of goods for more than a certain amount, which amount varies in different states, must be in writing, or there must be actual delivery and acceptance of the goods, or part payment must be made for them.

c.   A contract must be in writing to charge the defendant upon any special promise to answer for the debt, default, or miscarriage of another person or to charge any executor or administrator upon any special promise to answer any debt or damages out of his own estate.

d.   A written contract is necessary to charge any person upon any agreement made upon consideration of marriage, or upon any agreement that cannot be performed within the space of one year from the making thereof.

10.   DAMAGES FOR VIOLATION OF CONTRACT—A statute that provides no penalties for the lawbreaker is merely the expression of a wish or the giving of advice. Similarly, a contract must be binding on both parties. This element of mutual obligation is the very essence of a contract. The following are general rules that apply to violations of contracts:

a.   Where no actual loss has been sustained by the violation of a contract, the plaintiff is entitled to nominal damages only. For example, A contracts to drill a well for B and to complete same within a specified time or forfeit $1000, said amount being intended not as an assessment of the damages that would probably be actually sustained, but to secure the performance of the contract by the imposition of a penalty. The courts will not compel A to pay the $1000 to B. They will, however, permit B to recover from A such damages as he actually sustained as a result of A's failure to complete the well within the specified time.

b. Expected profits on speculations in real property cannot be recovered in case of a violation of contract.

c. Failure on the part of the seller to convey real estate or deliver personal property according to agreement entitles the plaintiff to recover damages or to sue for specific performance of the contract.

d. In case of loss of goods by a common carrier, the plaintiff is entitled to the value of the goods where they were to be delivered, less the freight on such goods.

e. If a party contracts to employ another for a certain time, at a specified compensation, and discharges him without cause before the expiration of the time, the employee can obtain judgment for the full amount of wages for the entire unexpired balance of the time, provided he is unable to secure employment in the same line of work after making an earnest effort to do so. Should he obtain work at a lower wage he can collect the difference.

f. To prevent lawsuits and disputes the amount of damages for the violation of contracts is sometimes fixed by the parties themselves by inserting in the contract some such provision as the following:

And it is further agreed that the party that shall fail to perform this agreement on his part shall pay to the other the full sum of (here state amount), as liquidated damages.

11. FORM:

GENERAL FORM OF CONTRACT

This agreement, made and entered into this . . . . . . day of . . . ., 19 . . . ., by and between Clarence Ranck of Aurora, County of Kane, State of Illinois, party of the first part, and Charles Vandersall of Columbus, Ohio, party of the second part, witnesseth:

In consideration of (insert consideration), it is agreed between the parties hereto as follows:

Said party of the first part agrees (insert agreement of party of the first part).

Said party of the second part agrees (insert agreement of the party of the second part).

In witness whereof the said parties have hereunto set their hands and seals the day and year first above written.

CLARENCE RANCK	(Seal)
CHARLES VANDERSALL	(Seal)

Copyright

1. DEFINITION—A *copyright* is the exclusive right to reproduce, publish, and sell a literary or artistic work. Under the United States copyright law, a copyright may be granted for the following classes of material:

a. Books, including collections, anthologies, and encyclopedias.
b. Magazines and newspapers.
c. Lectures, sermons, and other addresses for oral delivery.
d. Dramatic and musical-dramatic compositions.
e. Musical compositions.
f. Maps.
g. Works of art, including models and designs.
h. Reproductions of works of art.
i. Scientific or technical drawings or plastic work.
j. Photographs.
k. Prints and pictorial illustrations.
l. Motion-picture photoplays.
m. Other motion pictures.

Copyrights can also be secured on compilations, abridgments, arrangements, and adaptations, whether of non-copyrightable material or, with the permission of the copyright holder, of material that has been copyrighted already. Republished works that include new material are also copyrightable.

2. HOW TO OBTAIN—To secure a copyright on a work that is to be reproduced for sale or public distribution, the work should be published with a copyright notice, which may be in the following form:

Copyright © 1960
by
Jones, Smith, and Company

On maps, photographs, pictures, and other works where it is difficult to place a complete copyright notice, the letter *C* enclosed in a circle, ©, is used; it must be accompanied by a symbol or mark of the owner of the copyright, and his name must appear elsewhere on the work. After publication of the work, two copies of the best edition, or one copy, in the case of a work by a foreign citizen that was first published in another country, should be sent to the Copyright Office, Washington, D.C., with an application for registration. Books by American authors and proprietors or by alien authors and proprietors domiciled within the United States must be accompanied by an affidavit stating that the typesetting, printing, and binding were done in the United States. Forms for the affidavit and application for registration are supplied by the Copyright Office upon request.

3. FEES—The fee for registration of a published work is $6; payment of this sum also entitles one to a certificate under seal of the Copyright Office. The charge for the renewal of a copyright is $4. Copyrights may be assigned to other persons.

4. How to Obtain a Copyright for Other Articles—A copyright may also be obtained on certain works not published or reproduced for sale by filing an application for registration; the fee is $6. The application should be accompanied by one manuscript of the work, if it is a lecture, sermon, address, or dramatic or musical composition; by one print, for copyright of a photograph not intended for general circulation; or by a photograph or reproduction in the case of works of art, scientific or technical drawings, or plastic works. To obtain a copyright on a motion picture photoplay not published or for sale, the application for registration must be accompanied by the title, description, and a print from each scene or act. An application for registration of another type of motion picture must be accompanied by the title, description, and two prints from different sections of the picture.

5. DURATION OF COPYRIGHT—A copyright is valid for 28 years and may be renewed for the same length of time, provided application for renewal is made and registered within one year prior to the expiration of the original term of copyright. It cannot be renewed again. If an author is not living, his copyright may be renewed by the widow, the widower, or the children. If none of these are living the executors have the right of renewal, and if there is no will the copyright may be renewed by the next of kin. The person to whom a copyright has been assigned may also renew it at the expiration of the original 28-year period.

6. PRINTS AND LABELS—Copyrights may be taken out on prints and labels for advertising purposes. They first must be published with a notice of copyright. Application for registration would then be filed by the owner or author.

These copyrights are also effective for 28 years and may be renewed for a similar period.

7. UNIVERSAL COPYRIGHT—The United States is a party to the Universal Copyright Convention that became effective in September 1955. There are over fifty-five contracting states to this convention.

Under the terms of the agreement each state provides for the protection of the rights of authors and other copyright owners in literary, scientific, and artistic works, including writings, music, drama, cinematographic works, paintings, engravings, and sculpture. Works first published in any member nation will generally get the same protection in other member nations as they afford their own nationals. The copyright symbol © accompanied by the name of the copyright owner and the date of publication is sufficient to obtain protection for the work in any country that is a party to the Universal Copyright Convention.

Foreign works need not fulfill the United States requirement of deposit and registration if they are first published in a country party to the Universal Copyright Convention or if they are written by nationals of any of the contracting states.

8. APPLICATIONS for registration of claims to copyright are filed with the Register of Copyrights, Library of Congress, Washington, D.C. 20025. These application forms as well as information circulars covering the various subjects are furnished free upon request to the Register of Copyrights. Changes to the copyright law, proposed by the Subcommittee on Patents, Trademarks, and Copyrights of the Senate Committee on the Judiciary, may be obtained from the U.S. Government Printing Office.

Corporations

1. DEFINITION—A *corporation* is a group of persons empowered to act as a single individual, and treated by the law as such in many respects.

2. KINDS OF CORPORATIONS—*Business corporations,* engaged in enterprise to earn profit, are the most common. *Public corporations* are agencies of the government. Railroad corporations and other public service corporations, though performing a public service, are nevertheless *private corporations.* Then there are *religious, charitable and beneficial corporations,* usually organized for beneficial purposes, not for profit. *Quasi corporations,* such as school districts, resemble corporations in some ways. They can own and manage real estate, make contracts, sue and be sued

like any other corporation. A *close corporation* is one whose capital stock or ownership is confined to one family or distinct group of individuals.

3. FORMATION OF A CORPORATION—The formation of a corporation involves numerous legal questions, and should never be attempted without the services of a competent corporation lawyer. In most states the first step after having a certain amount of stock subscribed and paid for is to file with the secretary of the state a statement giving name, object, amount of capital stock, amount of stock paid for, location of office, and duration of the proposed corporation. The charter is then issued and a meeting of stockholders is called to elect directors. State laws vary, but usually three or more individuals may form a corporation. Corporations created in one state may transact any lawful business in another state, and they can acquire and transfer property as individuals, provided they comply with the law of the state in which they do business and obtain a license to do business there.

4. LIFE OF A CORPORATION—A corporation exists until the expiration of its charter unless it fails or is discontinued for other good reasons. Most charters are now perpetual. The stockholder's rights may pass from one to another by sale or by inheritance.

5. CAPITAL STOCK—Corporations generally have assets composed of money, real estate, buildings, machinery, patents, copyrights, etc. Capital stock is divided into parts called *shares*, and the owners of the shares are called *stockholders* or *shareholders*. By sale of shares the necessary money for the enterprise may be collected from many different sources, and unlike members in a partnership, the individual stockholders are not personally liable for the debts of the corporation. In large measure these facts account for the great popularity of the corporate form of organization. Corporations may increase or decrease the amount of their capital stock, provided the change is made in good faith without intent to defraud. See SECURITIES LAW.

6. WHO MAY SUBSCRIBE FOR STOCK—Anyone capable of making a contract may subscribe for the stock of a corporation. Minors are excluded. Where fictitious subscriptions are used to induce others to buy, the purchaser may refuse to pay his subscription; he may recover the money already paid, or he may keep the stock and sue for damages. The selling of subscriptions to stock is now very strictly regulated by statute.

7. THE STOCK CERTIFICATE is a written statement of the number and par value of the shares to which the holder is entitled. In other words, it is the evidence of ownership. A

stockholder may prove ownership even though a certificate has never been issued him. When the capital stock of a corporation is increased, each shareholder usually has the right to purchase a portion of the new stock before it can be offered for sale to outsiders.

8. PREFERRED STOCK – This kind of stock takes preference over the ordinary or common stock of a corporation. The holders of preferred stock are entitled either to a stated percentage annually out of the net earnings of the corporation before a dividend can be declared on the common stock or to some other preference set out in the certificate. Preference, rather than actual payment, is guaranteed. Holders of preferred stock usually have the right to vote at any stockholders' meeting on the same basis as the holders of common stock. In some states, the law requires that each share of stock have equal voting rights with every other share.

9. COMMON STOCK – The ordinary stock of a corporation is called common stock. The holders are entitled to all the rights incident to their ownership.

10. TRANSFER OF STOCK – This is provided for by statute. Usually the seller must assign the certificate to the transferee, execute a power of attorney, and deliver the certificate to the company for cancellation. The transfer agent then issues a new certificate to the purchaser.

11. SUBSCRIPTION – A subscription for stock is a contract and must be in writing. An agent cannot refuse to receive a subscription from a competent person, nor can he release a subscriber or alter the terms of the contract. The subscriber must inform himself as to his obligations and cannot evade payment unless he can prove fraud.

12. THE SHAREHOLDER'S LIABILITY — As stated previously, a corporation differs from a partnership in that the shareholders in a corporation are liable only for the amount of stock they own, while each member of a partnership is liable for all the debts of the firm. However, in the case of national banks the shareholders are liable for double the amount of their holdings in case the bank fails, if that much more is required to pay the debts. The amount of a stockholder's liability is fixed by statute. A stockholder in any corporation is liable for the full amount of his stock, whether paid in full or not.

13. RECEIVERSHIP — When a corporation fails, a receiver is sometimes appointed by the court to take charge of its affairs. The receiver has the power to convert the property into cash, levy and collect assessments from the shareholders, where authorized by law, and pay dividends to the

creditors, as in the case of bankruptcy proceedings (see also BANKRUPTCY). The receiver may be an individual, a group of individuals, or a trust company.

14. MANAGEMENT—The power of a corporation rests in its members or individual stockholders except as restricted or limited by law. Unless the charter or state laws alter the case, policies are determined by a majority vote; usually a shareholder has as many votes as he has shares in the corporation. The right to vote in a stockholders' meeting is determined by the stock record of ownership as of the date of meeting, or as of the date the books are closed prior to the meeting. The bylaws of the corporation generally fix the time for the closing of the books. A stockholder has the right to vote even if no certificate has been issued to him. He may vote in person or by proxy. An executor or trustee may vote the stock of the estate.

15. MEETINGS—The statutes or the bylaws of a corporation usually prescribe the manner in which meetings are to be called, and the bylaws fix the time and place of meetings. Should the proper officer fail to call a meeting at the required time, the meeting may lawfully be held later, and if he should refuse to issue the proper notice, he may be compelled by mandamus proceedings to do so. Regular meetings are held in the manner set forth by the charter or bylaws, and the object of the meeting need not be stated in the notice. On the other hand, special meetings may be called at any time on proper authority, but the notice must state the object of the meeting and no other business may be there transacted. Any authorized meeting may be adjourned from time to time or from day to day, and the adjournments must be considered as the same meeting. Even if a meeting is illegally called it becomes a valid meeting by ratification of the proper official or by the shareholders. Notice of meeting is sent to whoever has the right to vote the stock.

16. DIRECTORS—Management of a corporation is vested in the directors. Most corporations delegate managerial powers to directors who are elected either by a majority vote of the shareholders or by a cumulative system of voting in states in which such system is used. Their powers are established by statute, charter, or bylaws. As a rule they have general supervision over the business of the corporation. Their authority may be delegated to committees, corporate officials, or individuals. Thus the president, the secretary, the treasurer, and other officers and committees of the corporation are chosen by the board of directors to act in the capacity of agents in administering corporation affairs. A director may not act for the corporation individually, but his

unauthorized acts would bind the corporation if subsequently ratified. A director may not act both for the corporation and for himself in the same transaction. Unless otherwise provided, directors are not entitled to compensation for their services.

17. THE DIRECTORS' LIABILITY—The directors of a company are liable to the company and to shareholders and outsiders for negligence, fraud, or for acts committed outside the scope of their authority. These are questions of fact to be determined by the courts. The directors of a corporation are personally liable for its debts if it can be proved that they incurred the obligations knowing that the corporation was insolvent. They have been held personally, jointly, and severally liable as partners for debts of the corporation contracted in a state in which the company was found to have been doing business without having taken out a license.

18. OFFICERS—The officers of a corporation are usually the president, vice-president, secretary, and treasurer chosen by, and often from, the board of directors. The ordinary rules of agency govern their powers and duties.
a. The *president* is the chief executive officer and usually presides at meetings of the board of directors.
b. The *vice-president* takes over the duties of the president when, for any reason, the latter is unable to perform them. Quite frequently there are numerous vice-presidents assigned to different duties.
c. The *secretary* is the keeper of the records and the chief clerk of the corporation. He usually has the custody of the corporate seal.
d. The *treasurer* has charge of the corporation's finances. He is usually under bond for the faithful performance of his duties.

19. DIVIDENDS—A dividend is a payment to the shareholders out of the net profits of the corporation. A dividend may not be paid out of stated capital, but may be paid out of capital surplus. It may be in actual cash, in property, or in additional stock. When stock is selling above par on the exchange, corporations sometimes grant shareholders the right to purchase additional stock at par instead of declaring a cash stock dividend. The law will not permit the payment of dividends out of capital or from borrowed money without the consent of the stockholders, and the directors would be liable for such a fraudulent payment. Furthermore, illegally paid dividends may be recovered for the benefit of creditors. The net profit of a corporation is an asset, and not secure against creditors until the money has been declared as a dividend. When the dividend has been

legally declared payable, no action can be brought by creditors to stop its payment. The directors must act in good faith, but they cannot be compelled to pay dividends when they do not deem it advisable to do so. The courts hold that dividends must be general on all stock of the same class, so that each shareholder in that class will receive his just share, and that the dividends shall be paid to the owner as determined by the books of the company.

20. LIABILITIES OF A CORPORATION—Through its agents or servants a corporation can be guilty of slander, libel, false representation, trespass, or negligence, and can be sued accordingly.

21. THE SHAREHOLDER'S RIGHTS—In most states a shareholder has the right to inspect the company's books at any reasonable time for any proper purpose. Furthermore, he may employ an expert accountant to go through the records if he has reason to believe that the affairs of the company are not being handled properly. This right is limited in some states. In Illinois, for instance, the stockholder must either own 5 percent of the stock or have been a shareholder for six months in order to inspect the books.

22. FORMS—These forms relate to voting by proxy in a corporation.

GENERAL PROXY

Know all men by these presents, that I, ..., the undersigned, do hereby constitute and appoint . . . . my attorney and agent (with power of substitution for me and in my name, place and stead) to vote as my proxy for the election of directors and upon all matters that may be considered at the annual meeting of the stockholders of the . . . . company, to be held at its office at the city of . . . ., of the county of . . . ., state of . . . ., on the . . . . day of . . . ., 19 . . . ., at . . . . . o'clock . . . . .M., or any adjournment thereof, according to the number of votes I should be entitled to vote if I were personally present at said meeting, hereby revoking all former proxies by me made and given.

In witness whereof, I have hereunto set my hand and seal this . . . . day of . . . ., 19 . . . .

Witness:

. . . .   (Signature)

REVOCATION OF PROXY

Know all men by these presents, that I, the under-signed, do hereby revoke and annul a certain proxy by me given to .... (or, any and all prox-ies or powers of attorney heretofore given by me) authorizing and empowering the said .... to represent me and to vote in my name and stead and to act for me in any way whatsoever at any meeting or meetings of the stockholders of the ....
.... company.

In witness whereof, I have hereunto set my hand and seal this .... day of ......, 19 ....

(Witnessed)   (Signed)

Criminal Law and Procedure

1.   DEFINITIONS—A *crime* is an act in violation of some existing prohibitory statute and the common morality of the country. An individual cannot compromise a criminal wrong, for crime is a matter for the state to settle. Crimes may be classified as *felonies,* or more serious offenses, and *misdemeanors,* or less serious offenses, but the distinction is largely an arbitrary one.

2.   BURDEN OF PROOF—The burden of proof is upon the state. In other words, a person accused of a crime is pre-sumed to be innocent until the contrary is proved. Most states require that the verdict of the jury be unanimous to convict. If any reasonable doubt remains in the minds of the jury after it has heard all the evidence, it is its duty to ac-quit the defendant. Once acquitted, a prisoner cannot be brought to trial a second time for the same offense in the same jurisdiction.

3.   DEFENSES—Two defenses that are often raised are the defense of insanity and that of self-defense. A person who cannot distinguish right from wrong is insane and cannot be held responsible for his acts, but the insanity must be proved. Also, a person may defend his person, family, or property and may use such force as is necessary. If a person can show that the act was committed in self-defense he is guilty of no crime.

4.   CONFESSION—A legal confession must be voluntary and free from all compulsion, either physical or mental. Third-degree methods are unlawful, and a confession pro-cured by the use of threats or violence has no standing in court.

5.   TRIAL BY JURY—A person accused of a crime is guaranteed the right to a fair and impartial trial by a jury

(see JURIES) and the right to be represented by a competent lawyer. The trial must occur in the county where the crime was committed unless a change of venue is granted. The defendant is entitled to a change of venue if it can be proved that on account of prejudice on the part of the judge or jury the accused could not receive a fair trial in the county where the alleged crime was committed.

6. HABEAS CORPUS—A writ of habeas corpus is sometimes issued by the court to prevent people from being unlawfully deprived of their liberty. The prisoner is brought before the court and is released unless cause can be shown for his detention. This is a fundamental right under the Constitution.

7. CRIMINAL PROCEDURE—The first step in criminal procedure in most states is generally the issuing of a warrant by a justice of the peace or other judicial officer. When arrested, the accused is either placed in custody or, if he can furnish a satisfactory bond, released on bail awaiting trial. *Bail* means the sureties who bind themselves to have the accused present in court when required for trial. If the offense is a misdemeanor the case is usually tried and settled before the justice. If it is a felony, the justice holds a preliminary trial, certifying his findings to the grand jury. Acting in an investigating capacity, the grand jury may indict the accused, and the case is tried on its merits in the regular criminal court. If the grand jury fails to indict, the charge may be dropped on account of insufficient evidence.

8. CRIMINAL LAW IN BRIEF—The acts described in the following list are violations of criminal law in most states.

Accessory to the Crime. Any person assisting another to commit a crime or to escape from the scene of the crime is equally guilty with the principal.

Adultery. In many of the states, it is a crime for any married person to live openly with any person of the opposite sex who is not his lawful spouse.

Assault and Battery. A person who threatens or attempts to strike another person is guilty of assault, even though the threat is not followed by actual battery. Assault becomes battery when injury is actually done. The slightest unlawful touching may be battery.

Bigamy. A person having more than one husband or wife at one time is guilty of the crime of bigamy.

Bribery consists in the offering or giving of money or other valuable consideration to a public officer or one performing a public duty, as an inducement for him to commit an unlawful act. The giver and the receiver of the bribe are equally guilty.

Burglary consists in the unlawful breaking into and entering of the building of another with the intent to commit a crime.

Conspiracy. When two or more persons agree to do an unlawful act, the agreement is called a conspiracy, and is in itself a crime.

Contempt of Court. Any attempt to obstruct justice or to injure the dignity of the court is punishable by the action of the court.

Embezzlement is the wrongful appropriation and use of the personal property of another person by one to whom it has been voluntarily turned over for some lawful use.

Extortion is the asking and accepting of unlawful fees by a public officer.

False Pretense. It is a criminal offense to obtain money or other things of value by the false or fraudulent representation of a past or existing fact.

Forgery is the false making, or the material alteration, of a written instrument, contract, or any other legal paper with intent to defraud.

Fornication is illicit sexual intercourse other than adultery, as that between unmarried persons. It is punishable in some states.

Larceny is the unlawful appropriation and use of a person's property. It differs from embezzlement in that the original taking is unlawful.

Malicious Mischief is a crime that consists of the willful and intentional injury of another's property.

Manslaughter is the unlawful killing of a human being without malice or premeditation.

Mayhem is the act of maiming, disfiguring, or cutting away any part of the human body.

Murder is the unlawful taking of a human life with malice and premeditation.

Offenses on the High Seas are tried by the country under whose flag the ship is sailing.

Perjury is the false swearing of a person under oath. A person inducing another to perjure himself is equally guilty.

Rape. It is a felony to have sexual intercourse with a girl or woman without her consent.

Robbery is stealing property from another by force and intimidation. It is a felony punishable by imprisonment in the penitentiary.

Seduction. To have intercourse with a woman of chaste reputation through false promises of marriage is a crime.

Stolen Property. It is a crime to buy, receive, or conceal stolen property with the intent not to return it to the rightful owner. When buying property the buyer should demand proof of ownership.

Treason. It is treason to make war against, or to assist the enemies of, the existing government. Treason is punishable by death. A foreigner, owing no allegiance to the government, cannot be guilty of treason.

Unlawful Assembly. It is a criminal offense for two or more persons to assemble in contemplation of some unlawful act.

Deeds

1. DEFINITIONS—A *deed* is a written document conveying real estate. There are two kinds of deeds in general use: warranty deeds and quitclaim deeds. Any person of legal age, competent to transact business and owning real estate, may convey it by deed. The seller is called the *grantor,* the buyer the *grantee.* See also REAL ESTATE TRANSACTIONS.

2. A WARRANTY DEED is one in which the seller or grantor warrants the title to be good, and agrees to defend the same against all parties. Such a deed usually provides (a) that a seller has a right to convey the real estate, (b) that he is the owner of the land mentioned in the deed, (c) that the land is free and clear from all former and other grants, bargains, sales, liens, taxes, assessments, and encumbrances of any kind, and (d) that the purchaser will have quiet enjoyment of the real estate; that is, that he will not be put out of possession by anyone having superior title. If it afterwards develops that the grantor did not have the right to sell, or if the grantee discovers an encumbrance on the land, or if he has any trouble about the title, the purchaser has a good cause of action against the seller.

3. A QUITCLAIM DEED conveys only what interest the grantor may have in the property. This form of deed is often given by one whose title to the real estate may be defective. A quitclaim deed contains no warranties; the seller conveys only whatever interest he may have.

4. GENERAL PRINCIPLES:

a. Deeds must be written, typewritten, or printed.

b. The names of the parties and places of residence are generally written first.

c. The property must be fully described. The description should be by bounds, or by divisions of United States surveys, or by subdivisions into blocks and lots, as shown on the records in the county recorder's office.

d. The deed must express a consideration, and be signed

and sealed by the grantor or grantors. A deed without consideration is void.

e. Numbers should always be written in words followed by figures in parentheses, thus, Two Hundred Dollars ($200).

f. If the grantor is married, both husband and wife should join in the deed, and it should be executed and acknowledged by both.

g. The acknowledgment of a deed can be made only before persons authorized by law to take the same, such as justices of the peace, notaries, masters in chancery, and judges and clerks of the courts.

h. The deed takes effect upon its delivery to the person authorized to receive it, and should be recorded at once.

i. After the signing and acknowledgment of a deed the parties have no right to make the slightest alteration.

j. A person should never purchase real estate without a careful examination of the title by a trusted attorney.

k. Before advancing money or signing a contract for purchase of land or lots, the buyer should always procure an abstract of title or guaranty policy. See REAL ESTATE TRANSACTIONS.

l. A deed in which a mistake has been made can be corrected in all cases of fraud or accident.

m. In investigating the title to real estate, the attorney is bound to make a careful examination of the records and report the facts and his conclusions with respect to the condition of the title, and is liable for any injury resulting from his negligence.

n. A deed is considered recorded as soon as it reaches the recording officer, who generally notes upon it the day, hour, and minute when it was received by him.

o. If the land is a gift and no price is paid for it, it is customary to insert the words "in consideration of one dollar and other good and valuable considerations."

5. FORMS

WARRANTY DEED

Know all men by these presents, that we . . . . and . . . ., husband and wife, in consideration of the sum of $ . . . . in hand paid, do hereby grant, bargain, sell and convey to . . . ., of . . . . county, ..., the following described real estate situated in the county of . . . ., and state of . . . ., to wit: (describe premises), to have and to hold to his heirs and assigns forever. Together with all of the tenements, hereditaments, and appurtenances thereto belonging. And we hereby covenant with said .... that we are lawfully seized of said premises; that they are free from incumbrances; that we have good right and lawful authority to sell the same, and we covenant to warrant and defend the same against the lawful claims of all persons whosoever. And the said .... hereby relinquishes her right of dower in said premises.

In witness whereof we have hereunto set our hands and seals this ...... day of ...., 19 ....

In presence of   ....(Seal)

....(Seal)

State of ....
.... County.

            ....
            ....

On this .... day of ...., 19 ...., before me, a notary public in and for said county, personally came the above named .... and ...., his wife, who are known to me to be the identical persons whose names are affixed to the above deed as grantors, and severally acknowledge the instrument to be their voluntary act and deed.

In witness whereof I have hereunto set my hand the day and year above written.

            ....

Notary Public

Note: Statutes in many states provide for a short form which may be used in place of the above and has the same effect.

QUITCLAIM DEED

The grantor (here insert name or names of grantor or grantors and place or places of residence), of the city of ...., for the consideration of (here insert consideration), convey and quitclaim to (here insert name or names of grantee or grantees) all interest in the following described real estate (here insert description), situated in the county of .... in the state of ....

Dated this .... day of ...., A.D. 19 ......

       ...... (Seal)

Note: Use same form of acknowledgment as that shown for warranty deeds above.

Discrimination in Employment

1. INTRODUCTION—Title VII of the Civil Rights Act of 1964 prohibits employment practices that discriminate because of race, color, religion, sex, or national origin. The law applies to employers who have twenty-five or more employees, to employment agencies, and to labor organizations.

2. UNLAWFUL PRACTICES OF EMPLOYERS—It is an unlawful employment practice for an employer to fail or refuse to hire or to discharge any individual, or otherwise to discriminate against any individual with respect to his compensation, terms, conditions, or privileges of employment, because of such individual's race, color, religion, sex, or national origin.

3. UNLAWFUL PRACTICES OF EMPLOYMENT AGENCIES—It is an unlawful employment practice for an employment agency to fail or refuse to refer for employment, or otherwise to discriminate against any individual, or to classify or refer for employment any individual, on the basis of or because of his race, color, religion, sex, or national origin.

4. UNLAWFUL PRACTICES OF LABOR ORGANIZATIONS—It is an unlawful employment practice for a labor organization to exclude or to expel from its membership, or otherwise discriminate against, any individual because of race, color, religion, sex, or national origin.

5. EMPLOYMENT PRACTICES NOT IN VIOLATION OF THE LAW—The act specifically refers to the following practices as not constituting a violation of the law:

a. Any discrimination based on religion, sex, or national origin where religion, sex, or national origin is a bona fide occupational qualification reasonably necessary to the normal operation of that particular business or enterprise.

b. A policy by a church-supported educational institution to hire only employees who have certain religious beliefs.

c. Any discrimination based on a seniority, merit or incentive system or other like reasons that are not the result of any intention to discriminate because of race, color, religion, sex, or national origin.

Examples of unlawful practices include

a. Certain "male only" job classifications.

b. Wage differences between men and women doing the same work.

c. Not granting maternity leave to pregnant employees.

d. Nonequalization of male and female retirement ages.

e. Separate male and female seniority lists.

f. Allowing men but not women to smoke at their desks.

Dower

1. DEFINITIONS—*Dower* is the provision that the law makes for the support of a widow out of her deceased husband's estate. Unless modified by statute, this interest consists of the use for life of one-third of her husband's land after his death. During the husband's life, the law protects the wife's interest by prohibiting the sale of real estate unless she joins with him in signing the deed. If the property is sold and she does not sign the deed, she still has her dower right in the property. The interest that a husband acquires in the land belonging to his wife after her death is called *curtesy*. In some states the term *curtesy* has been abolished and the word *dower* substituted, so that the latter term applies to the interest of either the husband or the wife in the land of the deceased spouse.

2. GENERAL PRINCIPLES—The dower right is regulated by widely differing statutes in the several states. If the land is subject to a prior lien or to a mortgage that was signed by the wife along with her husband, the wife cannot get possession until the encumbrance has been removed. A woman may release her dower right by signing with her husband a deed for the conveyance of the real estate. A husband can will his wife a certain amount in place of her dower, but the wife can claim the dower instead if she prefers it. The widow is usually entitled to administer the estate of her deceased husband. Dower exists in growing crops and trees, and also in mines and quarries opened during the husband's lifetime. The widow of a partner is entitled to her dower in the partnership land after payment of all debts of the partnership. A legal marriage is necessary to sustain a dower estate. An absolute divorce divests the wife of her dower if the divorce was granted to the husband by reason of the wife's misconduct. Dower is assigned to the widow either by direction of the court or by agreement. Dower may be barred by a marriage settlement or agreement made before marriage.

Drunkenness

1. INTOXICATION—Both the civil and criminal courts are frequently called upon to rule on cases in which one of the parties involved was intoxicated.

2. GENERAL PRINCIPLES—It is the duty of those who deal

with an intoxicated person to take his condition into consideration. A sober party must exercise a reasonable degree of care to avoid injury to a drunken individual. A railroad company is also bound to take into account the helpless condition of its passenger, and to exercise reasonable care in keeping him out of danger. Drunkenness is not a legal excuse for the commission of a crime, but sometimes it is evidence of the absence of malice.

3. IN CIVIL CASES the courts have recognized cases in which intoxication was an excuse for repudiating a contract. The mental condition must be taken into consideration, especially where a man has become utterly incompetent or insane as a result of his intemperate habits. As we have seen before, such a man cannot make a contract. If one party is visibly intoxicated, the contract could be declared void on the ground that the other party must have realized his condition. The element of fraud enters if one party deliberately induced the condition of the other. However, if the intoxicated party ratifies the agreement when sober, or fails to repudiate it, he would be legally bound by it.

4. IN CRIMINAL CASES the courts hold that one who voluntarily becomes intoxicated cannot claim his intoxication as an excuse for his criminal acts. Yet in all such cases the facts must show intent to commit the crime before there can be any conviction. This aspect has been brought up in many cases where the defendant was so drunk that he entered the wrong house, or carried off the property of others, or slandered the reputation of another. Voluntary intoxication is a defense only where intent is an element of the crime.

Employer and Employee

1. EXPLANATION—The term *employee* refers to a person who is hired by a contract of service to perform certain duties for another person, called the *employer*.

2. KINDS OF CONTRACTS—There are two types of general employment contracts: (a) contracts to do some particular thing such as to buy and sell stocks or provisions, or collect accounts, and (b) contracts to do whatever the employer may direct. Farm hands, domestic servants, and clerks belong to this second class. Such contracts are frequently verbal, or even only implied, rather than written.

3. COMPENSATION—If no agreement has been made beforehand, the employee is entitled to the wages usually paid for such service. If the employee leaves because of insufficient food, ill-treatment, or disabling sickness, he is entitled to payment for the time he worked.

4. DUTIES OF EMPLOYEE—The employee is expected to perform faithfully the services for which he contracted for the entire term or period of service. In many cases, as in those of workers employed by the day or hour, this period of service may be very short. Courts frequently hold that if an employee leaves before expiration time, he can claim no pay for the work done. Some judges have held, however, that even in this case the employee is entitled to pay for work done, less what the employer lost by necessity of paying higher wages to the employee's successor, or what he lost by the employee's failing to perform his contract. The employee is bound to take reasonable care of the property in his care, and is liable for any loss or injury to it when due to his negligence.

5. DISCHARGE—An employee may be discharged at the end of his contract without any cause or previous notice. If he is discharged without good cause before the termination of his agreement, however, he is entitled to pay for the whole period, provided he has first made an earnest attempt to secure other employment in the same kind of work. If he gets work at lower wages, he is entitled to the difference. If his pay is equal to, or higher than, the former rate, he cannot collect. If, however, the discharge is on account of incapacity, dishonesty, or misconduct, he is not entitled to any pay for the unexpired period. Frequently a person is hired for a month, or for a year, at the termination of which the work continues. In such cases the law presumes a new contract on the same terms.

6. LIABILITY OF EMPLOYER—An employer's liability is of two kinds: (a) liability for the acts of his employees, and (b) liability for the injury or death of his employees.

7. LIABILITY FOR ACTS OF EMPLOYEE—The employer is liable for the wrongful acts of his employee producing injury to others, provided the acts are done in the course of the ordinary employment. Thus a railroad company is liable to passengers for negligence of conductors and engineers.

8. LIABILITY FOR INJURY OF EMPLOYEES—Workmen's compensation acts have largely provided new remedies to take the place of the employee's right to sue his employer for injuries incurred in the course of his employment. Under these acts liability is generally imposed upon the employer without regard to the question as to whether or not the employer was at fault, and payments are made as insurance rather than as damages.

9. WORKMEN'S COMPENSATION—Any person employed by a contract of service who is under the control of the employer while at work at the machine or other device from which the injury arose is entitled to compensation. Previous

physical condition is not considered in determining the amount.

10. WHO IS EXCLUDED—The workmen's compensation acts differ in the several states. The federal act protects persons employed by the United States and workmen engaged in interstate commerce. While it is difficult to give a general rule, the following are excluded from the benefits in most states, and in others the compensation is optional:

a. Minors and apprentices.
b. Farm laborers.
c. Domestic servants.
d. Casual employees.
e. Independent contractors.
f. Public officers.

11. DEPENDENTS—The law also provides that the compensation be paid to dependents in case of death. Payments may be made only to actual dependents or to partial dependents in accordance with the degree of dependency. These include widows, children, stepchildren, illegitimate children, adopted children, or a dependent parent.

12. PAYMENTS—The compensation acts provide for payments to the injured or his dependents in case of partial incapacity, permanent incapacity, or death, in amounts depending on the earning power of the injured at the time of the accident. Maximum and minimum amounts are usually specified.

13. INSURANCE —The compensation laws are rigidly enforced, and to protect themselves employers often take out liability insurance on the life and health of each employee. Then, when an accident occurs, the insurance company assumes all liability and relieves the employer of any claims that might be made under the workmen's compensation law. This method of limiting liability is provided for in the laws of all the states. The cost of such insurance is based on the size of the payroll and the nature of the employment. It ranges from a purely nominal figure for office work to a rather high rate for the more hazardous occupations.

14. VARIATIONS—It is impossible in a brief space to attempt an explanation of the workmen's compensation laws in the different states. In some states deductions are made for contributory negligence; in others, awards are fixed for specific injuries; and in almost every state there can be found numerous variations.

15. SOURCES OF INFORMATION—Copies of the compensation and liability statutes may be secured free of charge by writing to the Secretary of State of the state for which information is desired. He should be addressed at the state

capital. Owing to the technical nature of the subject, however, it is always a good plan to ask an insurance adviser to explain the duties and obligations under the law.

16. THE FAIR LABOR STANDARDS ACT—In 1938 Congress enacted the Fair Labor Standards Act, which set a minimum wage and maximum workweek for employees engaged in interstate commerce or in the production of goods for commerce. Because of the broad interpretation by the Supreme Court of the federal government's constitutional power to regulate interstate commerce, this act has a widespread effect on employment.

There are also provisions in the act restricting the employment of children. Children under eighteen years of age may not engage in hazardous occupations. Children under sixteen years may work for their parents in nonmining or nonmanufacturing occupations. Children between the ages of fourteen and sixteen years may work at nonmining and nonmanufacturing occupations after school hours and under conditions that will not affect their health or wellbeing.

The Fair Labor Standards Act is administered by the Wage and Hour Division of the United States Department of Labor at Washington, D.C. Many of the states have similar legislation affecting employment conditions among employees working in business wholly within the state.

17. THE NATIONAL LABOR RELATIONS ACT AND LABOR-MANAGEMENT RELATIONS ACT—The National Labor Relations Act, known as the Wagner Act, has given employees the legal right to organize and bargain collectively with their employers without interference or coercion by the employers. The National Labor Relations Board enforces the act and may, upon request of the employer or employees, hold an election to determine which union shall act as bargaining agent. The Board may prohibit the employer from using unfair labor practices and may, after proper hearing, compel the reinstatement of a former employee discharged because of union activities. The act has been amended by the Labor-Management Relations Act known as the Taft-Hartley Act, which has added such things as prohibitions against unfair labor practices by employees. Some states have legislation patterned after these acts.

18. THE NORRIS-LA GUARDIA ACT—Another federal act affecting employer-employee relationships is the Norris-La Guardia Act, which restricts the power of the federal courts to issue injunctions in labor disputes, although these restrictions have been eased somewhat by the Taft-Hartley Act, and prohibits them from enforcing "yellow dog" contracts.

A *yellow dog contract* is one by which the employee, as a condition of his employment, agrees to withdraw from, or refrain from joining, a labor organization. Some states have similar laws affecting their own courts.

19. THE SOCIAL SECURITY ACT—The two phases of the Social Security Act that are most important to employer and employee are: (a) that which sets up a permanent system of old-age benefits, and (b) that which promotes the enactment of permanent unemployment insurance systems by the states. The old-age benefit system is administered by the federal government, and to support the plan, employer and employee pay a tax based on the size of the employee's wage, which the employer must remit to the federal treasury. When the employee reaches 65, his monthly benefit payments begin and their amount is calculated with reference to the total tax he has paid over his years of work. These benefit provisions apply to all classes of persons within the act, and should not be confused with old-age pensions to needy persons.

The act attempts to induce the states to enact and administer unemployment insurance systems. The employer must pay a tax on his total payroll into the federal treasury. If the state has an unemployment insurance act that meets the standards set up by Congress, the federal government will grant money to the state to help pay the cost of the insurance. The employer may also deduct up to 90 per cent of the federal tax to pay the state unemployment insurance tax.

Other sections of the Social Security Act provide for federal grants to the states for maternal and child welfare, for public health work, and for aid to the blind, the needy aged, and dependent children. Medicare and Medicaid programs are also administered under the Social Security Act. See MEDICARE.

Equitable Remedies

1. DEFINITION—A *remedy* is the legal means employed to enforce a right or redress an injury. Suppose A has purchased an automobile from B who refused to deliver it. In a court of equity A could compel B to deliver the car; this would be an equitable remedy. In a court of law A could recover damages for the loss he had sustained through B's refusal to deliver the automobile; this would be a legal remedy.

2. THE COMMON REMEDY—Relief in equity is often sought to compel a person to execute a contract that he has made. It quite frequently happens that a seller regrets his

action after the contract has been made. The court of equity will compel him to deliver the property, provided that the law gives the purchaser no adequate remedy. When an article has a peculiar sentimental value, when it is of rare value, like an heirloom, or when it is an article that cannot be easily purchased in the open market, the one party can compel the other to fulfill his contract. Ordinarily, the buyer of articles like cattle, lumber, dry goods, or hardware has only the legal remedy to recover damages.

3. CONDITIONS FOR RELIEF BY EQUITY — Equity will enforce agreements or grant relief:

a. When legal remedies or damages would be inadequate.
b. When the seller of a business agrees not to enter into competition with the buyer.
c. When an employee agrees not to disclose the trade secrets of his employer.
d. When a tenant threatens or attempts to injure the real estate of the landlord.
e. When an established patent has been infringed.
f. In many other similar cases.

4. EQUITY WILL NOT ENFORCE AGREEMENTS OR GRANT RELIEF:

a. When the law has an adequate remedy.
b. When the goods contracted for can be readily purchased in the open market.
c. To force a person to perform his contract to render personal services.
d. When the contract in question is one where one party agrees to lend money to the other.
e. When there is a contract to form a partnership.
f. When such agreement would be in restraint of trade, would create a monopoly, or would be illegal for any other reason.

5. INJUNCTIONS — Relief in equity is often brought about by the means of an injunction. An *injunction* is a restraining order issued by a court of equity on petition of the injured party. If the need is great the court will immediately issue a temporary injunction that orders the injuring party to do, or not to do, certain things, and fixes the time for a hearing. At this hearing, which is fixed within a reasonable time, and which is conducted like any ordinary trial, the court decides whether the injunction will be dissolved or whether it will be made permanent. Injunctions came into especial prominence through their use against labor unions during strikes. Injunctions were issued and upheld enjoining the members of labor unions from picketing, or otherwise preventing other workers from taking their places. Legislation

has curbed the use of injunctions against labor groups although they are still legal in some cases.

Exemptions

1. DEFINITIONS — *Exemption* is a right granted to debtors, especially bankrupts, that protects the homestead or other property from the claims of creditors. A *homestead* is the abode or dwelling house of a family landowner and includes a specific amount of the adjacent land, varying in the different states. *Exemption laws* protect those who are unable to pay their debts without causing distress to themselves and their families.

2. GENERAL PRINCIPLES — The laws in some states provide that a person can waive his exemption rights in a promissory note or other written contract. The laws of other states provide that exemptions cannot be waived. In nearly all the states an exemption in wages cannot be waived. A legal homestead is generally in one piece, but it may be divided by a road and in some states may consist of several distinct pieces. A homestead is exempt from all debts except taxes, although in some states it is not exempt from pre-existing liens, fines for public offenses, and similar debts. A person who is the head of a family, within the legal meaning of the term, is generally entitled to homestead exemption. This right survives to the husband or the wife in case of death, or to the surviving children until they come of age. In divorce cases the wife ceases to be a member of the family and thus loses her homestead right unless reserved in the decree. Desertion of the husband by the wife does not destroy his homestead right but does destroy hers. A homestead may be sold or mortgaged regardless of the claims of creditors.

Guaranty

1. DEFINITIONS — A *guaranty* is a written promise that a person will perform some duty or contract, or answer for the payment of some debt, in case of the failure of another person. The person who guarantees the faithfulness of another is called the *guarantor*. The *guarantee* or creditor is the person to whom the pledge is made.

2. GENERAL PRINCIPLES:

a. A guaranty must be in writing.

b. A guaranty, to be binding, must be for a consideration.

c. A guaranty must be accepted in order for it to become a contract, and the guarantor must have notice of its acceptance within a reasonable time.

d. A guarantor, after paying the debt, can become the legally recognized creditor of the person for whom he was guarantor.

3. FORMS:

GUARANTY ON BACK OF A NOTE

Fort Scott, Kansas, Oct. 12, 19 . . . . .

For value received, I hereby guarantee the payment of the note.

JAMES GLOVER

GUARANTY FOR PAYMENT OF A BILL

Dayton, Ohio, Aug. 30, 19 . . . . .

W. Reinke, Esq.

Dear Sir:

I hereby guarantee the payment of any bill or bills of merchandise Mr. John A. Dahlem may purchase from you, the amount of this guaranty not to exceed Five Hundred Dollars ($500), and to expire at the end of three months from date.

CHAS. ADAMS

GUARANTY OF A DEBT ALREADY INCURRED

St. Louis, Mo., July 10, 19 . . . . .

Messrs. H. E. Bechtel & Co., West Salem

Gentlemen:

In consideration of One Dollar ($1) and other good and valuable considerations paid me by yourselves, the receipt of which I hereby acknowledge, I guarantee that the debt of Four Hundred Dollars ($400) now owing to you by Ira J. Ferry shall be paid at maturity.

W. A. PIPER

Infants

1. DEFINITIONS—While the word *infant* in its ordinary usage signifies a child of a tender and helpless age, the word *infant* as used in law refers to a person who has not arrived at his majority as fixed by law. *Majority* is the age at which the disabilities of infancy are removed, and hence a person who has reached his majority is entitled to the management

of his own affairs and to the enjoyment of civic rights.

2. NATURE OF INFANCY—The disabilities of infancy are in fact personal privileges conferred on infants by law, and as such they constitute limitations on the legal capacity of infants, not to defeat their rights but to shield and protect them from the acts of their own improvidence as well as from acts of others.

3. TERMINATION OF INFANCY—Under the common law, infants, whether male or female, attain their majority at the age of 21 years, and this rule has generally remained in force throughout the United States, unless changed by statute. As a result of the new equal protection decisions and the Twenty-sixth Amendment to the federal Constitution lowering the minimum voting age to 18, there is a nationwide trend to establish the age of 18 as the termination of infancy for both males and females. The period of incapacity arising from infancy is limited by law, and cannot in any case be enlarged or diminished by evidence.

4. EMANCIPATION—An infant may be emancipated by an act of his parent, or by his marriage, or by his enlistment in the military service. While parental emancipation or emancipation by marriage or by enlistment affects the parent's rights and obligations to the infant, such emancipation does not otherwise remove the incapacity of his infancy or affect the avoidability of his contracts.

5. REAL ESTATE—An infant is capable of taking title to real estate granted to him by a deed.

6. PROGRESSIVE CAPACITY—While a person is an infant in the eyes of the law until he arrives at the age of majority fixed by law, his actual capacity to do acts involving legal consequences and the practical necessity of his doing such acts increases from babyhood to the age of majority, and the law necessarily recognizes such progressive capacity. Thus, subject to certain conditions provided by statute, an infant over a certain age may select his own guardian, or may enter into a valid and binding marriage, or may enlist in the military service.

7. RIGHT TO REPUDIATE COMPROMISE OR SETTLEMENT—If a compromise or settlement of an infant's claim or cause of action is made on his behalf by a third person, such as his parent, he may repudiate such agreement before reaching his majority or within a reasonable time thereafter, unless it is made by a guardian with authority to do so or is otherwise approved by a court.

8. CONTRACTS—The prevailing rule today is that, in the absence of a statute to the contrary, an infant's contracts or conveyances are voidable, with the exception of certain

limited classes of contracts or transactions that are valid and binding. This rule is applicable to both executed and executory contracts, although in some cases it is held that the infant is bound by the term of his employment contract to the extent that he has executed it without dissent.

9. TORT LIABILITY—The general rule is that an infant is liable for his own torts in the same manner and to the same extent as an adult, if the tort does not arise out of, or is not connected with, a contract. Infancy is not a shield against tort liability except to the extent that infants are incapable of forming the mental attitudes that are necessary elements of certain torts. Thus, an infant may be held liable for injuries caused by his negligence, and ordinarily infancy cannot be pleaded as a defense in an action for fraud, for assault and battery, or for trespass.

10. NEGLIGENCE—In determining whether an infant is guilty of actionable negligence, the standard of care applicable to him is the standard of a child of similar age and experience. According to some recent cases, however, this rule is not applicable when a minor engages in such adult and potentially dangerous activities as the operation of an automobile or other motor-powered vehicles, and a minor operating such a vehicle or craft is to be held to the same standard of care as an adult. Whether or not a minor has been negligent under a particular set of circumstances is ordinarily a question of fact, although infants of very tender years, usually seven or under, may be conclusively presumed incapable of negligence.

Innkeeper

1. DEFINITION—An *innkeeper* is one who keeps a public house for the reception and entertainment of travelers.

2. GAINING ADMISSION TO AN INN OR HOTEL—An innkeeper is required to accommodate all comers with the following exceptions, which vary in different states:

a. He may exclude anyone if he has no accommodations.

b. He may exclude those who do not come at a suitable time or in a proper manner.

c. He must exclude certain persons such as criminals and thieves.

d. He may refuse admission to those he believes would disturb the peace and safety of his guests.

e. He can expel any guest who does disturb the peace and safety of his other guests.

If he refuses to provide reasonable and proper accommodations, he is liable. He need not provide any particular room. If he operates a garage or stable in connection with the inn, he is under the same obligation to receive and care for the automobiles or horses of his guests.

3. THE INNKEEPER'S LIABILITY —The law fixes the liability and responsibility of an innkeeper:

a. An innkeeper is responsible for the loss or damage to a guest's baggage committed to his care unless such loss is caused by an act of God, a public enemy, or neglect or fault of the owner of the baggage.

b. In most states innkeepers are relieved from liability for loss by fire unless the fire is caused by the negligence of the innkeeper or his servants.

c. An innkeeper is liable for goods of a guest if they were stolen by the innkeeper's servants, by another guest, or by an outsider. However, he is not liable if the loss was due to the negligence of the owner.

d. The innkeeper is bound to secure honest and trustworthy employees.

e. If two guests occupy the same room, the innkeeper can be held responsible if a theft is committed by one against the other.

4. LIENS—An innkeeper has a lien on a guest's baggage or other property left in his care, to secure the payment for the accommodations.

5. REGULATIONS—An innkeeper may make regulations for the observance of his guests in order to protect their property. Thus he may limit his liability somewhat by notifying the guests that he is not responsible for the loss of valuable articles unless they are deposited with him. Such regulations will bind the guest if brought to his notice.

6. LODGING AND BOARDING HOUSES—The keepers of lodging or boarding houses do not come under the same head as innkeepers as far as the law is concerned. They are not required to accommodate all who may apply. They are not liable for refusing to accommodate all comers.

Insurance

1. DEFINITIONS—*Insurance* is a contract stating that one party, the *underwriter,* will compensate another party, the *insured,* for any damage to a specific thing caused by a specified danger or for liability incurred under certain circumstances. Insurance contracts are called *policies.* The consideration paid by the insured to the underwriter is called the *premium.* Fire insurance and life insurance are two important basic kinds of insurance.

2. FIRE INSURANCE—*Fire insurance* is indemnity against loss by fire. That is, the underwriter agrees to reimburse the

insured for damage caused to the insured property by fire.
Thus it provides a means of distributing the cost of damages
caused by fire. A fund is supplied by the payment of premiums, from which the insurance company agrees to pay
the loss in case of fire. Fire insurance is now generally furnished by large stock companies or by mutual companies.

3. MUTUAL COMPANIES are generally established by
statute and provide for the payment of losses by pro rata
assessment upon the policyholders, who constitute the
stockholders and who manage the affairs of the company. In
effect, each member of a mutual company gains protection
for his insured property and accepts a small part of the risk
of the other members. Some of these mutual companies require a small premium paid in advance, which, unless
unusual losses occur, is enough to pay all the losses for the
year. Others simply require a small fee to pay for the expense of making the survey and issuing the policy. In case of
loss, all mutual companies, however, make an assessment
pro rata upon the policyholders to pay the same.

4. STOCK INSURANCE COMPANIES — The insurance business of private corporations is carried on for profit.

5. GENERAL PRINCIPLES — The following general principles apply to property and fire insurance.

a. The property insured, and the terms of the contract,
    must be clearly defined.

b. If the written part of the policy contradicts the printed
    sections, the written part will hold.

c. Clerical or typographical errors may usually be cor-
    rected when discovered.

d. The insurance on the building covers those things that
    have become a part of it, but does not include fixtures or
    surrounding sheds or buildings.

e. Misrepresentation or fraud on the part of the insured
    renders the insurance policy null and void.

f. If a policyholder secures additional fire insurance on
    his property without the consent of the insurance com-
    pany, his former policy becomes void. Most policies to-
    day, however, consent to the writing of additional in-
    surance on the property by other companies and in case
    of loss the liability is prorated.

g. In addition to the actual fire loss, most policies cover
    damage by water used to put out the fire, damage to
    goods while being removed to avoid fire, and damage
    from an explosion caused by fire.

h. An insurance company is not responsible for goods
    stolen while they are being removed during a fire.

i. An ordinary policy of insurance does not usually insure

against lightning, but lightning clauses will be attached to nearly all policies if requested at the time of issue.

j. The insurance company is not relieved from liability by the carelessness of the policyholder, yet the insured is bound to take reasonable care to prevent fire.

k. In a total loss the insurance company is liable for the full value of the property, provided that this value does not exceed the amount of the insurance. In a partial loss the company is liable only for the actual loss.

l. In an *open policy* the amount of the insurer's liability is not fixed until after the loss. In a *valued policy* the maximum liability for a total loss is fixed.

m. In order to calculate the approximate loss on merchandise in case of fire, the value of the following items should be ascertained: (1) the most recent inventory; (2) invoices for goods bought subsequent to that inventory; (3) freight and dray bills on same; (4) credit memoranda for merchandise returned; (5) production department payrolls; and (6) appreciation in value of goods since purchase. These items should be added together and from their sum should be subtracted the sum of the following items: (1) outgoing charges, representing goods sold since the last inventory; (2) depreciation in value of goods since purchase; and (3) salvage, or market value, of goods not destroyed. The remainder gives the approximate value of goods destroyed, for which insurance compensation can be obtained.

6. UNDERWRITERS' ASSOCIATIONS—The stock fire insurance companies all submit complete underwriting and loss figures to the National Board of Underwriters, which, in addition to compiling and publishing such information, supervises common services to the public, such as fire protection, information, and grading. There are also local agents' boards and state associations operating to promote uniformity of service and contract. Fire insurance rates are usually established by rating bureaus, which are administered and paid for by a majority of companies doing business in the state or locality. Rates are usually adhered to by all agents either by common agreement or as directed by state law. Specific rates are published for mercantile houses, warehouses, office buildings, and manufacturing buildings. Rates by classes are used for dwellings, small apartment houses, farms, and similar property.

7. CLASSIFICATION—In order that each person thus protected from loss may contribute the proper amount to this fund, a system of classification has been worked out to establish fair premium rates. This classification is based on

the probability of fire. The National Board of Fire Underwriters, having the reports of the various insurance companies, knows the probable number of fires and the value of
the property involved. Statistics show that a certain percentage of residences, barns, schools, merchandise, etc., will be
burned each year, and that buildings of one type of construction are more likely to burn than those of some other
type of construction. Population, water pressure, fire department, building contents, and many other elements are
taken into consideration by the rating bureau in determining the rate each person must pay for insurance.

8. REDUCING THE RATE—When you pay your premium,
you can judge by the rate you pay what the experience of
the insurance companies has been with regard to similar
property, with similar conditions. If the rate is high, find out
just what factors make it high. Then you may be able to
make such changes or take such precautions that your rate
will be reduced.

9. WHO HAS AN INSURABLE INTEREST—In order to be in-
demnified against loss the insured must have an interest in
the property or goods insured, both at the time the insurance is issued and at the time of the loss. Thus the following may be insured:

a.   A bailee (one who receives goods of another to hold).
b.   A consignee (one to whom property is consigned or
     shipped).
c.   A mortgagee (one who holds a mortgage on real or per-
     sonal property).
d.   An assignee (one to whom property is assigned).
e.   A warehouseman.
f.   An executor or an administrator.
g.   A landlord.
h.   A tenant.
i.   The holder of a lien on property.
j.   An agent who has the custody or care of the principal's
     property.

All these as well as many others have what is called an insurable interest. If all insurable interests in a property are
not noted on the policy at the time of loss, the company is
not liable to the party having an interest which is not so
noted.

10. THE INSURANCE POLICY is a contract between the insurance company and the insured, by which the first party
insures the property of the second party against loss by fire.
The consideration, or premium, is usually paid when the
policy is issued, although it may be charged on account or
paid by check or note. The contract becomes binding and
valid when the policy is properly executed. Actual delivery

of the policy to the insured is not necessary. Thus if a loss occurs after the duly executed policy is in the hands of the insurance company's agent, but before it has been delivered to the insured, the company must pay the loss. A preliminary contract is sometimes made, in which case the risk, that is, the liability of the insurance company, begins immediately upon the signing, even though such contract be dated several days before the policy is actually issued. Most local agents have authority to protect an applicant for insurance against loss for a period of 5 to 30 days preceding acceptance of the risk by the company.

11. CANCELLATION—A fire insurance contract, like any other contract, may be canceled by mutual agreement, but unless otherwise stated in the policy the company cannot cancel the contract without the consent of the policyholder.

12. LIFE INSURANCE—*Life insurance* is a contract whereby the insurer agrees, on the payment of a fixed premium, to pay a certain sum of money to the insured when he reaches a certain age, or to his beneficiaries at his death. Thus it is possible for a man to insure his productive ability for the amount of money it would be worth to him if he were to live for his expected time.

13. APPLICATIONS—Nearly all companies require applications for life insurance to be in writing and accompanied by the report of a medical examination made by the local medical examiner of the company. These applications are forwarded to the home office and, if they pass the head medical examiner, the policy is issued to the insured and the application is made a part of the policy. Any false statement contained therein that is material to the risk will vitiate the policy, and applicants for insurance should be careful to see that all questions are fully and truthfully answered. The moral hazard involved is also carefully considered by the insuring company. Most life insurance policies provide that the insurance shall not be in force until the first premium is paid, and most policies are now incontestable after the payment of a certain number of premiums. By the laws of all states, in case default is made in the payment of a premium after a certain number of full premiums have been paid, the policyholder may have the option to select any one of the following nonforfeiture provisions:

a. Cash surrender value.

b. Reduced paid-up insurance.

c. Term insurance for the full face amount of the policy.

14. GENERAL PRINCIPLES—The following general principles apply to life insurance.

a. Unless forbidden by statute, a life insurance policy may

be assigned to one having an insurable interest, or to a person without such an interest, provided that the assignment is made in good faith. An assignment is often made for the benefit of creditors, or as security for the payment of a debt.

b. A contract for insurance does not take effect until it has been approved by the company, and the insured has paid the first premium.

c. A general agent can bind his principal even against the express terms of the policy provided that the insured was not negligent in failing to advise himself concerning the terms.

d. A life insurance contract may be void on account of a mistake in issuing it, on account of violation of statute, on account of fraud by either party, or if the policy is contrary to public policy.

e. Words or figures written or printed on the margin or on the back of the policy, or on a slip attached to the policy, must be considered as an integral part of the agreement.

f. The payment of premiums to an agent will bind the company, unless the insured has received notice to the contrary.

g. A policy may be canceled by mutual agreement, and the insured is then entitled to the surrender value of the policy or any other nonforfeiture option contained therein.

15. THE POLICY—The usual clauses contained in life insurance policies are these: (a) that the insurance ceases unless the premiums are promptly paid, (b) that the company shall be exempt if, within two years after the issuance of the policy, the insured commits suicide whether sane or insane, or if death shall come by the hands of justice for a violation of law, (c) that agents are not authorized to alter or discharge any part of the contract, (d) that assignments of the policy shall not take effect until notice thereof shall be received by the company at its home office, (e) that after two years the policy will be incontestable except for fraud or nonpayment of premium. All policies also provide for a 30- or 31-day period of grace after the due date for payment of premiums.

16. INSURABLE INTEREST—In order for an insurance policy to be valid the person taking out the policy must have an insurable interest in the subject matter of the insurance, that is, the policyholder must be one who would suffer loss, financial or otherwise, on the happening of the event insured against. However, such a person may name any bene-

ficiary, although companies hesitate to approve applications for life insurance where the named beneficiary has no such interest. The relationship of uncle or aunt and nephew or niece, or that of cousins is generally not sufficient unless other circumstances show an insurable interest.

17. KINDS OF POLICIES—There are many kinds of life insurance policies. Among the more common are the following:

a. *Ordinary Life Policy* in which premiums are paid during life and in which the face value of the policy is payable at death. This is the simplest and lowest-premium form of life insurance.

b. *Limited Payment Plan*—The face value of the policy is payable only at death, and premiums are payable only for a limited period of years, or until death if it occurs within that period.

c. *Endowment Policy*—The insurance company agrees to pay a fixed sum at the end of a fixed term of years, or at death, if it occurs before the expiration of the term, provided a fixed premium is paid during the entire term.

d. *Convertible Term Policy* insures against death for a limited term of years, and may be converted into any other form of insurance, without medical examination, within a stated period.

e. *Income Agreements* may be issued on any of the other plans, with a provision that the face value of the policy is to be paid in monthly installments instead of in a lump sum.

18. AUTOMOBILE INSURANCE—The owner of a car may be held liable for damage done by his vehicle, even when someone else is driving it. And damage done to his automobile and its occupants, either through collision or by some other cause, may be expensive. To protect himself against financial loss related to his automobile, the owner may take out an automobile insurance policy. Automobile insurance is of four kinds: liability, collision, comprehensive, and no-fault.

a. *Liability Insurance* protects the owner, up to the limits stated on the policy, against liability for damage done by his automobile through fault of an authorized operator. Such insurance policies cover property damage done to other cars and expenses for personal injury to occupants of the insured vehicle, to occupants of other cars, and to injured pedestrians. Since the law considers an automobile an inherently dangerous machine, many states require that an automobile owner must have liability insurance in order to register and license his vehicle.

b. *Collision Insurance*—Damage to the insured vehicle and injuries to its occupants are covered by collision insurance. If the operator of an insured vehicle is at fault in an accident, or if the insured vehicle is damaged through fault of an uninsured motorist, collision insurance will cover the owner's loss.

c. *Comprehensive Coverage* insures an automobile against damage not related to traffic accidents. The policy may cover loss by fire, theft, severe weather, vandalism, and falling objects, depending on the terms of the policy. It does not cover damages caused by collision.

d. *No-Fault Insurance*—Many court cases involve disagreements over which driver is at fault in an accident and what damages should be paid to injured parties. These cases may involve much time and great expense. In order to reduce the load on the courts and the cost of liability insurance, some states are instituting forms of *no-fault insurance*. No-fault insurance imposes on the owners of motor vehicles a limited liability, without regard to fault, for personal injuries or death caused by the operation of their motor vehicles. It can be considered a form of strict liability similar to workmen's compensation. See EMPLOYER AND EMPLOYEE: WORKMEN'S COMPENSATION.

   19.   OTHER FORMS OF INSURANCE:

a. *Accident Insurance* may be secured against all kinds of accidents. Upon payment of small premiums, policies may be had insuring against accident from one day to ten years, for any reasonable amount. The rates generally depend upon the occupation of the insured.

b. *Marine Insurance* is governed largely by the same rules that control fire insurance. This form of insurance may include all casualties resulting from unusual or violent actions of the elements, foundering at sea, grounding, collision, fire, perils of war, rests and restraints, jettison, and any other perils, losses, or misfortunes of the sea.

c. *Fraternal Insurance* is one of the oldest forms of insurance, originating with the ancient secret societies. Originally the societies assumed an obligation to pay sick and death benefits to their members. Today there are numerous societies that issue standard life insurance policies, with a fixed premium rate and a limited amount of insurance payable at death.

d. *Industrial Insurance*—Many large business organizations issue this form of insurance for the benefit of their employees. The amounts are usually small and the weekly or monthly payments are deducted from the wages of the insured.

e. *Other Kinds of Insurance* include employers' liability (see EMPLOYER AND EMPLOYEE: INSURANCE), public liability, tornado, explosion, health, hospital, automobile, burglary, fraud, insolvency, and loss through bad debts. Almost every kind of risk imaginable may be covered by insurance.

20. FORM:

ASSIGNMENT OF POLICY OF INSURANCE

Know all men by these presents, that I, ... of the village of ...., for and in consideration of ...., to me in hand paid by .... of the same place, the receipt whereof is hereby acknowledged, have sold, assigned, transferred, and set over, and by these presents do sell, assign, transfer, and set over, unto the said .... the policy of insurance known as policy No ..... of the .... Insurance Company, and all sum and sums of money, interest, benefit, and advantage whatsoever, now due, or hereafter to arise, or to be had or made by virtue thereof, to have and to hold the same unto the said .... and his assigns forever.

In witness whereof, I have hereto affixed my hand this 20th day of June, 19 ......

(Acknowledgment)   (Name)

International Law

1. DEFINITION—*International law* is the body of rules designed to govern the conduct of nations toward one another. It includes customs and usages that have grown up among nations and have become generally accepted by them as well as the enactments contained in treaties and conventions. International law is intended to do for nations what the domestic law does for individuals.

2. GENERAL PRINCIPLES—There are certain well-established principles of international law, which provide as follows:

a. One nation cannot interfere with the internal affairs of another.

b. Crimes committed on the high seas are under the jurisdiction of the nation under whose flag the ship sails.

c. The property of alien enemies is subject to confiscation.

d. A neutral country must be fair and impartial in its relations with warring nations.

e. It is a violation of international law for a warring nation to fight on, or cross the territory of, a neutral power.

f. It is also a violation of international law to carry the necessary finished goods or materials of warfare to a combatant nation.

g. A fugitive criminal cannot be brought back from another nation unless the terms of the treaty between the two nations so provide.

h. Confiscation is the penalty for attempting to violate a blockade in time of war.

3. TREATIES—Much international law is embodied in treaties. A *treaty* is an agreement between two or more nations to adjust differences or to govern future conduct. Treaties are sometimes made for a limited period of years, but a treaty made by one administration is binding upon the following administration.

4. REPRESENTATIVES—*Ambassadors* are the authorized diplomatic representatives of nations. They are immune from civil or criminal liability, but may be tried for crime by their home governments. A *consul* is a commercial representative sent by one nation to another to aid in the establishment and maintenance of trade relations between the nations, and to look after the interests of the citizens or subjects of his country. He is personally liable for his actions.

5. PASSPORTS—A *passport* is a document granted by the government to a citizen enabling him to travel to other countries. See PASSPORTS.

Juries

1. DEFINITION—A *jury* is a body of laymen selected by lot, or by some other fair and impartial means, to ascertain, under the guidance of a judge, the truth in questions of fact arising in either a civil or criminal proceeding. At common law a jury was composed of 12 persons summoned from the vicinity, duly examined and sworn to try the case on the facts presented by the evidence introduced at the trial.

2. FUNCTION OF JURY—In general terms, the province of the modern-day jury is the determination of questions of fact arising in the trial of the action in which it sits. A *jury trial* is a proceeding in which the jurors are the judges of the

facts and the court is the judge of the law. In early times, the jury served as a body of witnesses acting upon their own personal knowledge, but the accepted principle now is that the jury exercises its province upon the evidence introduced at the trial, not upon its own knowledge obtained elsewhere.

3. RIGHT TO A JURY TRIAL— The right to have a trial by jury is a fundamental right in our democratic system, and is recognized as such in the Magna Carta, the Declaration of Independence, the federal Constitution, and the constitutions of the various states. The Federal Rules of Civil Procedure also state that the right of trial by jury as declared by the Seventh Amendment to the Constitution, or as given by a statute of the United States, must be preserved to the parties inviolate. And the United States Code sets forth matters in connection with juries and trial by jury. While the right to a jury trial is guaranteed in the Constitution, the specific rules governing juries are somewhat flexible. A jury may be composed of fewer than twelve members, and a jury need not unanimously agree on a verdict. These matters are left to the discretion of the states.

4. FEDERAL CONSTITUTIONAL PROVISIONS— When the Constitution of the United States was amended to include the Bill of Rights, the people, by virtue of the Seventh Amendment, secured from general encroachment the right to trial by jury in all actions at common law in the federal courts where the value in controversy exceeds $20. This means that if the suit were of the kind which was triable as of right by jury in 1791, when the Seventh Amendment was adopted, it is triable as of right by jury today. Since the legal terminology has changed since the eighteenth century, it is necessary to look at the substance of the particular lawsuit to determine whether it is of the type triable by jury then.

One example that points up the contrast is workmen's compensation. This type of action was unknown in 1791 and no right of jury trial had therefore become attached to it. Thus there is no such right in the federal courts today in such an action.

5. APPLICABILITY TO STATE COURTS —The federal Constitution does not in any place expressly guarantee the right of trial by jury in any state court or in any territories which have not been incorporated into the Union.

6. STATE CONSTITUTIONAL PROVISIONS—The constitutions of the several states generally contain express guaranties of the right to a jury trial. The typical provision is that the right shall be and remain inviolate, or that the right, as heretofore enjoyed, shall remain inviolate. Such provisions apply to both civil and criminal cases. The right is secured, and not granted, by such a provision.

Lease

1. DEFINITIONS—The phrase *landlord and tenant* denotes the relationship that exists by virtue of a contract expressed or implied between two or more persons for the possession or occupancy of lands or tenements either for a definite period or at will. The landlord or *lessor* is the person who lets the land or premises. The tenant or *lessee* is the one who occupies the land or premises. The *lease* is the contract between the two.

2. LEASES SHOULD BE IN WRITING—Leases that are to remain in force for more than a year or that are not to be performed within a year must be in writing, or they are invalid. Leases for a year or less and that can be performed within a year are valid even if not in writing. To avoid misunderstandings, disputes, and possible litigation it is always best, however, that the lease be in writing and signed by both parties, regardless of the length of the term.

3. LEASES FOR LIFE are those that are terminated by death either of the lessee or of some other person living at the date of the lease. Unless such leases contain covenants to the contrary, the life tenant or the lessee is required to pay all taxes on the premises and keep the same in repair.

4. LEASES FOR YEARS—The lessor, unless it is otherwise expressly provided in the lease, is under obligation to see that his tenant's possession is not disturbed by any title paramount to the landlord's. He is not required to make repairs unless he agrees to do so in the lease, nor is there an implied contract on his part that the premises are fit for the purpose for which they are let. For residential leases, however, most states tend to interpret the lease as an implied covenant of habitability. The landlord must pay all the taxes regularly levied and assessed against said premises and keep the buildings on said premises insured at his own expense if he desires to carry insurance.

5. IMPLIED AGREEMENT BY TENANT—Where there is no agreement to the contrary, the tenant is bound to take possession of the premises, take ordinary care of the same, keep them in a tenantable condition, and make repairs made necessary by his negligence, but he need not make repairs made necessary by ordinary wear and tear or inevitable accident.

If the premises leased be a farm, he is also required to cultivate the same in the manner required of good husbandry. He must not commit waste nor alter buildings or fences, and must surrender up the premises at the end of his term in as good condition as when entered upon originally, ordinary wear and tear excepted. He is not required to pay taxes or keep buildings insured, but must pay the stipulated rent at the time it becomes due by the terms of his lease. If no time is specified in his lease, then the rent is due at the end of the term. He may sublet the premises or assign the lease unless it contains provisions to the contrary.

If he places permanent improvements upon the premises that are so attached to the buildings or land that they cannot be removed without injury to the buildings or land, he has no right to remove the same unless his lease so provides. He may remove trade fixtures, provided they are removed from the premises before the expiration of his lease.

6. COMMON PROVISIONS OF A LEASE—Most leases provide for the yielding up of the possession of the premises at the end of the term without notice, in as good condition as when they were entered upon by the lessee, loss by fire, inevitable accident, and ordinary wear excepted. There is frequently a provision against subletting or assigning the lease, and a clause stating that in case of nonpayment of rent, or failure to perform any of the covenants of the lease, the lessor shall have the right to terminate the lease and recover possession of the premises.

Farm leases usually provide, in addition to the stipulations mentioned above, that the tenant shall keep the fruit and ornamental trees, vines, and shrubbery free from injury by stock, plowing, or otherwise; that the lessee will draw out the manure and spread it on the premises; that no straw shall be sold or removed from the premises during the term or at its termination; that the tenant will keep the buildings and fences in repair, the landlord to furnish necessary material; that the landlord may do fall plowing on the stubble ground after the grain has been removed therefrom, and that he may enter for the purpose of making repairs or viewing the premises. Sometimes the landlord covenants to make all new fences, to furnish water, and to carry out other provisions that may be inserted in the lease.

7. TERMINATION OF LEASE—Under the strict rules of the common law the landlord might terminate the lease for nonpayment of rent, but in order to do so it would have been necessary for him to go upon the premises and make a demand for the exact amount of rent due upon the very day that the rent came due, and a failure to do this waived the right to obtain forfeiture. This strict rule of the common law has been modified in nearly all the states so that it is no longer necessary to make a demand for the rent on the day the rent comes due. Instead of this, most of the states provide that before the landlord shall declare a forfeiture, a

written demand for the amount of rent due shall be served upon the tenant, and he be notified that in case he fails to pay the rent within a fixed time, generally five or ten days, the landlord will elect to terminate his lease. In such cases the tenant has until the end of the last day fixed in the notice to pay the rent and prevent the forfeiture. The statutes of the various states also provide that in case of breaches of other agreements contained in the lease, notice of such breaches and intention of the landlord to terminate the lease shall be served upon the tenant.

8. TERMINATION OF TENANCY FROM YEAR TO YEAR AND MONTH TO MONTH—Where a tenant has a lease for a year, and at the end of his term remains in possession of the property without a new agreement, the law construes this to be a leasing from year to year, and such tenancy at common law could be terminated only by either party's giving the other six months' notice prior to the end of any year. In Illinois, this notice has been changed by a statute to sixty days prior to the end of any year, and a shorter time has been fixed in other states. A tenant who has a lease on property for one or more months and who remains on the property after the termination of his lease, is termed a tenant from month to month, and such tenancy can be terminated only by either party giving the other party thirty days' notice. A tenancy from month to month may also be created by agreement. A tenancy at will is one which can be terminated at any time by either party.

9. DEMAND—It is a general rule, subject to few exceptions, that in order to get possession of property where the original occupancy by the tenant was lawful, either a notice to quit or a demand for possession is necessary on the part of the owner before commencing proceedings to get possession.

10. SECURING POSSESSION—When a lease has been terminated either by its term or by notice, and the landlord is entitled to possession, the most common method of recovering possession is to commence an action of forcible entry and detainer against the tenant for the possession of the premises. This may be done by filing a complaint and having a summons issued. If the possession of the tenant was lawful at the time of its beginning, the landlord has no right to dispossess him forcibly, and if he does so it is at his peril. Taking possession by force may subject the landlord to an action for damages. Leases sometimes contain clauses stating that where a forfeiture has taken place the landlord shall have the right to take possession of the premises leased, by force if necessary. Such provisions, however, cannot be enforced and do not justify the landlord in using force. The only legal

course for the landlord is to begin an action, obtain a judgment for possession, and have the constable or sheriff put
him in legal possession.

11. DISTRESS FOR RENT—An effective method of collecting rent is by *distress warrant*. This is a warrant issued by
the landlord to some third person, authorizing and empowering such third person to levy said warrant upon any
personal property of the tenant for the satisfaction of the
rent. A very important advantage of this remedy is that it
enables the landlord to seize the personal property of the
tenant without delay. This process is of very ancient origin.
As used here the term *personal property* means property
other than real estate. The statutes of most of the states provide for this remedy, and the mode of procedure is generally
prescribed by the statute. In general, it is the duty of the officer, as soon as the levy is made, to file with a justice of the
peace or with the clerk of the court an inventory of the property levied upon, together with a copy of his warrant, and
usually a summons is issued.

12. TIME OF LEVY—Under the common law the tenant
had all of the day on which the rent came due to make payment, and a distress warrant could not be levied until the
day after the rent came due. In some states, however, in
case the tenant sells or attempts to dispose of the crop
grown upon the premises, thereby endangering the landlord's lien for his rent, a distress warrant may be levied
before the rent comes due. The person making the levy
should be careful not to levy on more property than is
necessary in order to satisfy the rent due; otherwise he may
be liable to the tenant for making an excessive levy.

13. LANDLORD'S LIEN—Under the common law the landlord had no lien upon the property of the tenant until a distress warrant was actually levied upon the property of the
tenant. Most of the states, however, now provide that the
landlord shall have a lien upon all the crops grown upon the
leased premises until the rent for the year in which said
crop was grown has been paid, and this lien is ahead of all
other liens, even though another legal claim may have been
levied upon such crops. The landlord's lien is paramount until the rent is satisfied. The usual method of enforcing the
lien of the landlord is by distress warrant.

14. COURT DECISIONS REGARDING RENT—The courts have
held that
a. Unless the tenant makes a specific agreement relieving
   himself, he is liable for the rent of the building on the
   land leased, after the building has burned down, just as
   if he were still occupying it.

b. When the terms of a lease are in doubt, the courts endeavor to ascertain the intention of the parties from the lease itself and from the circumstances under which it was made.

c. The term of a lease expiring on a specified day continues through the whole of that day.

d. When the tenant continues to occupy the premises without the consent of the landlord after the expiration of the lease, the landlord may treat him either as a trespasser or as a tenant for another term.

e. A lease may be made to take effect at some future date.

f. A lease must clearly define the property, but no special form or wording is necessary.

g. Valid leases may be made by minors, corporations, executors, administrators, or trustees, subject to certain restrictions. However, there is always uncertainty in a contract with a minor.

h. A lease for an unlawful purpose is generally held to be void.

i. As in other contracts, if the printed and the written parts of a lease do not agree, the written part will usually hold.

j. Most states are coming to interpret a lease as an implied covenant of habitability. That is, the lease of a private house is a warranty that it is fit to be lived in or occupied.

k. When a landlord agrees to keep the building in repair and fails to do so, the tenant's remedy is to sue for damages. He may not continue to occupy the premises and refuse to pay rent.

l. When a tenant is evicted he is excused from the payment of rent for any time after his eviction. Any act by the landlord that renders the property unfit for, or impossible of, occupancy is an eviction.

m. If land is rented on shares, the relation of landlord and tenant usually exists even if the rent is to be paid in produce instead of cash.

n. The landlord is liable for injuries caused by defective stairways, open elevator shafts, or other dangerous conditions that exist in the parts of a rented building that are under his control.

15. FORM:

SHORT FORM OF LEASE

This indenture, made this sixth day of April, 19...., between John Parks, as lessor, and J. B. Moulton, as lessee, witnesseth: That the lessor has this

day leased to the lessee the premises known as number 142 Archer Street, in the City of Chicago and
State of Illinois, to be occupied by the lessee as a
residence (or insert any other purpose for which building is leased) only, for and during the term commencing on the first day of May, 19 . . . . ., and ending on the
thirtieth day of April, 19 . . . ., upon the terms and conditions hereinafter set forth; and in consideration of
said demise and the covenants and agreements
hereinafter set forth, it is covenanted and agreed as
follows:

FIRST.—The lessee shall pay to the lessor at the office of the lessor as rent for said leased premises for
said term the sum of Six Hundred Dollars ($600) pay-
able in advance in equal monthly installments upon
the first day of each and every month during the term
hereof.

SECOND.—The lessee has examined said premises
prior to and as a condition precedent to his acceptance
and the execution hereof and is satisfied with the
physical condition thereof, and the lessee's taking
possession thereof shall be conclusive evidence of the
lessee's receipt thereof in good order and repair, except as otherwise specified herein, and the lessee
agrees to keep said premises and the appurtenances
thereto in a clean, sightly, and healthy condition and
in good repair, and to yield back said premises to the
lessor upon the termination of this lease, whether
such termination shall occur by expiration of the term
hereof or in any other manner whatever, in the same
condition of cleanliness, sightliness, and repair as at
the date of the execution hereof, loss by fire or other
casualty, and ordinary wear and tear excepted.

THIRD.—The lessee agrees to pay the water tax
charged against said premises when due.

FOURTH.—The lessee agrees to allow the lessor free
access to the leased premises for the purpose of examining or exhibiting the same, or making any need-
ful repairs or alterations of said premises which the
lessor may see fit to make; also to allow to be placed
upon said premises at all times during the term hereof
"For Sale" and "To Rent" signs and not to interfere
with the same.

FIFTH.—The lessee agrees not to assign this lease,
nor sublet said leased premises, or any part thereof,
without the written consent of the lessor endorsed
hereon.

SIXTH.—In case said leased premises shall be vacated

during said term the lessor may take immediate possession thereof for the remainder of the term and in his discretion relet the same and apply the proceeds upon this lease, the lessee to remain liable for the unpaid balance of the rent.

SEVENTH.—The failure of the lessee to perform the foregoing covenants, or any of them, shall constitute a forfeiture of all of the lessee's rights under this lease and the further occupancy by the lessee of said leased premises after such forfeiture shall be deemed and taken as a forcible detainer of such premises by the lessee, and the lessor may, without notice, re-enter and take possession thereof, with or without force, and with or without legal process, evict and dispossess the lessee from and of said leased premises.

EIGHTH.—The foregoing covenants, and the terms and conditions of this lease, shall inure to the benefit of and be binding upon the respective heirs, devisees, personal representatives, successors, and assigns of the parties hereto, except as herein otherwise provided.

Witness the hands and seals of the parties hereto, the day and the year first above written.

JOHN PARKS   (Seal)

....
Lessor

J. B. MOULTON   (Seal)

....
Lessee

Legal Remedies

1. DEFINITION—A *remedy* is a legal means employed to enforce a right or redress an injury. For example, suppose A and B enter into a binding contract for the purchase and sale of land. If A, the seller, refuses to live up to his contract, B can sue A for the damages he sustained through A's refusal to sell the land. This would be a *legal remedy*. If in a court of equity B could compel A to sell him the land, that would be an *equitable remedy*. See EQUITABLE REMEDIES.

2. STEPS NECESSARY TO SECURE A LEGAL REMEDY—When one party to a contract has a legal cause of action against the other, he brings suit as follows:

a. B files a complaint against A, stating the agreement and giving the facts of A's failure to fulfill his contract, and the loss resulting to B from such violation.

b. A is summoned to appear in court to answer the charge and the court is asked to render judgment against A for the damage resulting from A's refusal to fulfill the contract, and for the costs.

c. The case is then tried, and if judgment is rendered against A, the court empowers the sheriff to levy on any property A may have above statutory exemptions, sell it, and turn the proceeds over to B for the damages awarded, returning any surplus to A.

3. VARIOUS KINDS OF ACTIONS—The common-law forms of action have been abolished in most states, but similar actions are allowed by the codes that have supplanted the common-law forms of action. The following is a list of actions, for the most part designated and defined as they were at common law:

a. *Complaint* is the general name used in many states for the pleading used to institute any legal action.

b. *Ejectment* is a form of action to determine the title to land and right of possession.

c. *Habeas Corpus* is an action or writ used to recover a person's liberty from illegal restraint.

d. *Libel* is an action brought to collect damages for any malicious writing tending to injure the business or reputation of the plaintiff. Although malice is an element of libel, malice will be conclusively presumed even if the defamation was an accident.

e. *Mandamus* is an action to compel someone to do some specific thing pertaining to his office or duty.

f. *Quo Warranto* is a writ used to recover an office or a franchise from the person or corporation in possession of it.

g. *Replevin* is a form of action for the recovery of the possession of specific personal property.

h. *Slander* is an action to collect damages for malicious defamation by word of mouth.

i. *Tort* is an action to recover damages for a private or civil wrong or injury arising independent of any contract.

License

1. DEFINITIONS—A *license* is a right or permission granted by competent authority to a person, giving him the right to do something that otherwise he would not have the right to do. The *licensor* is the one who grants the license.

The *licensee* is the one to whom the license is issued.

2. KINDS OF LICENSES—Licenses are of almost infinite variety and are issued not only by the federal government, but by states, counties, cities, towns, and villages. They may be issued to manufacturers or dealers in certain articles, such as tobacco or liquor, to proprietors of amusement places, peddlers, transportation companies, chauffeurs, automobile owners, itinerant merchants, and cab drivers. Such licenses are issued under what is known as the police power of the state.

3. ILLEGAL LICENSES—Cities sometimes require the payment of a local license fee by salesmen or canvassers who are taking orders for goods to be shipped from another state at some future time. Such licenses are legitimate in themselves, but the Supreme Court has ruled that when the fees become excessive, this type of license operates as an undue restraint of interstate commerce and is therefore illegal.

4. MARRIAGE LICENSES—All states require a marriage license. The person who performs the ceremony is required by law to note the fact of the marriage on the face of the license, and to return it to the county recorder for record.

Lien

1. A LIEN is a legal claim upon property for the payment of a debt. It is the right to hold possession of property, usually until some claim against the owner has been satisfied.

2. POSSESSION is always necessary to create a lien, except in cases of mortgages and judgments and statutory liens such as mechanics' liens. The lien simply permits the holding of the property in question until the debt is satisfied. The property cannot be sold without the consent of the owner, except by order of the court.

3. LAW—The existence of a lien does not prevent the party entitled to it from collecting the debt or claim by taking it into court.

4. PARTIES ENTITLED TO LIENS —Warehousemen, carpenters, tailors, dyers, millers, printers, etc., or any persons who perform labor or advance money on property or goods of another, usually have a lien on that property or those goods until all charges are paid.

5. HOTEL KEEPERS have a lien on the baggage of the guests whom they have accommodated.

6. COMMON CARRIERS have a lien on goods carried for transportation charges.

7. AGENTS have a lien on goods of their principals for

money advanced.

8.   REAL PROPERTY—If the debt is on a house, barn or other real property, the creditor may file a lien on the whole property, and have it recorded in the county recorder's office. The claim then partakes of the nature of a mortgage.

9.   MECHANIC'S LIEN—Nearly all the states permit liens designed to protect certain classes of individuals, who furnish material and labor for the erection, construction, repair, and improvement of buildings. The method of securing these liens and enforcing them varies so widely in the different states that it is almost impossible to give such a statement as will cover all states. The courts have construed such laws very strictly, and in order to entitle a person to such lien the provisions of the law granting the same must be strictly complied with. Individuals desiring to avail themselves of these statutes should consult a lawyer and have him prepare the necessary papers.

10.   FORM OF MECHANIC'S LIEN—The following form is commonly in use in the state of Illinois:

STATE OF ILLINOIS,   )
COUNTY OF DU PAGE.) ss.
Julius Warren)
          vs.   )   Claim for Lien
Martin Smith)

The Claimant, Julius Warren, of the City of Wheaton, County of Du Page, State of Illinois, hereby files a Claim for Lien against Martin Smith of Du Page County, Illinois, and states:

That on the first day of October, 19 . . . ., said Martin Smith was the owner of the following described land, to wit: Lot two (2) in Block three (3) of the original town of Hinsdale, in the County of Du Page and State of Illinois.

That on the first day of October, 19 . . . ., the Claimant made a contract with said owner to furnish labor and materials for the building to be erected on said land for the sum of Seven Hundred Fifty Dollars ($750), and on the 23rd day of October, 19 . . . ., completed all work required to be done by said contract.

That said owner is entitled to credits on account thereof totaling Two Hundred Fifty Dollars ($250), leaving due, unpaid and owing to the Claimant on account thereof, after allowing all credits, the balance of Five Hundred Dollars ($500), for which, with interest,

the Claimant claims a lien on said land and improvements.

JULIUS WARREN

. . . .

STATE OF ILLINOIS,   )
COUNTY OF DU PAGE.) ss.
   Julius Warren, being first duly sworn, on oath
deposes and says, That he is the above named Claimant, that he has read the foregoing Claim for Lien.
knows the contents thereof, and that all the statements therein contained are true.

JULIUS WARREN

. . . .

   Subscribed and sworn to before me
this 1st day of November, 19 . . . .

GEORGE JOHNSON

. . . .
Notary Public

(Seal)

Marriage

1. MARRIAGE is a civil contract. Marriage licenses are required by all the states, and many restrictions concerning
the issuing of such licenses have been made within recent
years. Unlike other contracts, marriage cannot be terminated by the consent of both parties.
2. GENERAL PRINCIPLES--The following principles apply
to a contract of marriage.
a.   There must be a serious agreement or mutual assent of
     both parties.
b.   A marriage may be declared void because of fraud, in-
     competence of one of the parties, or the fact that one of
     the parties is underage.
c.   The legal age at which marriage can legally be con-
     tracted without parental consent varies from state to
     state. With consent of parents or guardians, the
     minimum age in several states is 18 for men and 16 for
     women; in states under common law the ages are 14 and
     12 respectively. As a result of the new equal protection
     decisions and the Twenty-sixth Amendment to the
     federal Constitution lowering the minimum voting age

to 18, there is a nationwide trend to establish the age of 18 as the legal age for both males and females.

d. A marriage is not void simply because it has been improperly performed or licensed, but the officials responsible are liable.

e. At common law a wife is solely responsible for her crimes unless they were committed in her husband's presence, in which case coercion on the part of the husband is presumed. In many states this law has been changed so that the husband is responsible only when he participated in the crime, unless coercion is proved.

f. A married man can sue for the alienation of his wife's affections. In some states the wife has a similar right. Suits for alienation of affections are now prohibited by the laws of a number of states.

g. Either husband or wife may act as the agent for the other party.

h. The husband is not responsible for the debts or wrongs of his wife unless, of course, the debts are necessary for the support of the family.

i. The husband must provide a home, and support and protect his wife and children. His duty to protect his family carries with it all the rights of "self-defense."

j. He must maintain law and order in his household, and may use force in preventing a member of his family from committing a crime.

k. A wife is required to care for the house and family. She cannot be forced to go into business or enter any gainful occupation.

l. The husband must support his wife, and she can pledge his credit for articles necessary to sustain life and maintain her social position.

3. A MARRIAGE CONTRACT—A marriage is a civil contract, and is entered into by the consent of the parties. If a man says to a woman, "Will you marry me?" or words to that effect, and she says "Yes," or words that imply an affirmative answer, it is, by law, an agreement or promise of marriage, and both parties are legally held to carry out in good faith the promise thus made. Mutual promise by a man and a woman to marry at some future day constitutes a valid contract in some states.

4. BREACH OF PROMISE—If either party refuses to carry out the contract, he or she is guilty of breach of promise, and in some states the other party may recover damages. It is not very often that the man sues the woman, though he has an equal right to do so if she fails to make good her promise. In several states, however, suits for breach of promise are now outlawed.

5. NECESSARY PROOF—Generally in case of a lawsuit for breach of promise, there are no direct witnesses, as people usually become engaged without the presence of a third party. The engagement may be implied from the conduct of the party sued.

6. IMPLIED EVIDENCE—In states where suit for breach of promise is recognized, a promise of marriage may be implied from circumstances such as constant visits, presents, open declaration of the parties, and their reception by the parents or friends as an engaged couple without any objections from the party being sued.

7. EXCUSES FOR BREAKING THE PROMISE—A refusal to marry may be justified on the ground of the bad character or conduct of the other party; poor health of either party is sometimes a good excuse, but not generally. If the woman were a widow or a divorcee and concealed this fact from the man, this justifies a refusal on his part to marry.

8. TIME OF MARRIAGE—When a man promises to marry a woman without stating any special time, the law may hold him guilty of breach of promise unless he is ready to fulfill his engagement within a reasonable time; five years was held in one instance to be an unreasonable time.

9. WHEN A PROMISE IS NOT BINDING —If either party is underage, he or she is not bound by promise to marry and the law will excuse the party underage.

10. SEDUCTION—Seduction of a woman under promise of marriage and subsequent refusal on the man's part to marry subjects him to damages in a civil action and often to criminal liability as well.

11. SEPARATION—The law allows agreements between husband and wife in which they agree to live separately. This does not in any way abolish the wife's rights in the husband's estate unless the contract so specifies.

12. DIVORCE—Divorces are of two kinds: (a) absolute divorces, and (b) judicial separation, generally known as separate maintenance. The word *divorce* as now commonly used has the former meaning. In the case of an absolute divorce the marriage is ended and the parties become single. A *judicial separation* is a limited divorce in which the court gives one party the right to live separately from the other. The decree of divorce usually makes provision for the payment of alimony, for the custody and support of any children, and for the settlement of property rights between the parties. The divorce laws of the several states vary, although most states recognize and respect the laws of the other states.

13. AUTHORITY OF WIFE LIVING APART FROM HUSBAND TO

BIND HIM—Whether or not the person who supplies a wife with necessaries has knowledge of her husband's provision for her support, the presumption of a wife's authority to pledge her husband's credit is negatived by the fact of their living apart, and the tradesman who supplies her under such circumstances upon the credit of her husband, and without the husband's express sanction or approval, does so at his own peril. In order to charge her husband with the cost of supplies furnished her, the tradesman must show not only that they were of the kind usually regarded as "necessaries," but that in consequence of the inadequacy of the husband's provision, they were actually required for the wife's proper support, commensurate with the husband's means and the wife's station in the community.

14. PROPERTY RIGHTS OF MARRIED WOMEN—Nearly all the states have enacted legislative provisions for the benefit of married women. These laws vary greatly in the different states, and there are frequent changes, but all tend toward the releasing of woman from her former condition of absolute dependence upon her husband. By the old common law a married woman had few rights. She was subject to the authority of her husband, and he could rule over her. This condition has now been changed, however, and the rights of married women are recognized by every court. All property owned by the wife before marriage, or received after marriage and held as her separate property, can be sold and transferred without the consent of her husband except his rights of dower or curtesy in her real estate. If a husband fails to make provision for the support of his wife, the law will compel him to furnish her proper support if he has sufficient means.

Medicare

1. DEFINITION—*Medicare* is a federal program of health insurance for the aged. The Medicare program enacted in 1965 provides a comprehensive medical benefit program administered by the Social Security Administration of the Department of Health, Education and Welfare. The two basic benefits are generally referred to as Hospital Insurance (Part A) and Medical Insurance (Part B), the first providing hospital, extended care and home health benefits and the second providing the services of physicians and ambulance, outpatient hospital and home health services.

2. ELIGIBILITY FOR HOSPITAL INSURANCE BENEFITS —Persons who have attained age 65 and are entitled to monthly insurance benefits under the Social Security system or who

are qualified railroad retirement beneficiaries are entitled to benefits under Part A. Disqualification to receive some or all of the retirement benefits by reason of earnings is not a disqualification to receive Part A benefits. Application for these benefits should be made within the three-month period before the person attains age 65.

3.   SCOPE OF HOSPITAL INSURANCE BENEFITS—For each benefit (spell of illness), a person is entitled to the following Part A benefits:

a.   Up to 90 days in a hospital.

b.   Up to 100 days of posthospital care in an extended care facility.

c.   Up to 100 visits for posthospital home health services, such as visits by nurses, therapists and health aides, during a one-year period following release from a hospital or extended care facility.

4.   BENEFIT PERIODS—A *benefit period* is a period of consecutive days beginning with the first day the individual is furnished inpatient hospital services or extended care services and ending with the close of the first period of 60 consecutive days in which the individual is not an inpatient of a hospital or of an extended care facility. There is no limit to the number of benefit periods that a person may have. Once a person enters a new benefit period he is entitled to a new round of benefits. In addition, each person has a "lifetime reserve" of 60 additional hospital days that can be drawn on for any days in excess of 90 that he remains in the hospital during any benefit period. These days are used automatically at the first opportunity unless the person specifies that he does not desire to use them.

5.   PAYMENTS—During each benefit period Medicare pays for all covered services for the first 60 days except a small initial amount—presently $60—which will increase with the annual rise in hospital costs. For the 61st through 90th day Medicare pays for all covered services except $15 per day. There are special rules for benefits in psychiatric hospitals including a lifetime reserve of 190 hospital benefit days.

6.   ELIGIBILITY FOR MEDICAL INSURANCE BENEFITS— Whereas those who qualify for Hospital Insurance under Part A and make application therefor are automatically eligible, the Medical Insurance benefits are available only to persons 65 years of age or over who elect to enroll in the program and who pay the premiums. An individual is eligible to enroll only if he has attained age 65 and (a) is a resident of the United States, either as a citizen or as an alien lawfully admitted for permanent residence who has resided

in the United States continuously during the five years immediately preceding the month in which he applies for
enrollment for medical insurance, or (b) is entitled to hospital benefits under Part A.

7. SCOPE OF MEDICAL INSURANCE BENEFITS—The services
covered by Part B include

a. Medical and surgical services by a doctor of medicine or
   osteopathy, wherever furnished.

b. Certain medical and surgical services by a doctor of dental medicine or a doctor of dental surgery.

c. Other services ordinarily furnished in a doctor's office.

d. Outpatient hospital benefits, including laboratory, diag-
   nostic, X-ray and radiology services, emergency room,
   and medical supplies.

e. Outpatient physical therapy services furnished under
   direct and personal supervision of a doctor or by a
   qualified hospital, extensive care facility, home health
   agency or public health agency and under a plan established and periodically reviewed by a doctor.

f. Up to 100 home health visits if all of the following are
   present: (1) the individual needs part-time skilled nurs-
   ing care or physical or speech therapy services; (2) the
   individual is confined to his home; (3) a doctor deter-
   mines that home health care is needed; (4) a doctor sets
   up and periodically reviews the plan for home health
   care; and (5) the home health agency is participating in
   Medicare.

8. LIMITATIONS—The medical services covered by Part B
are subject to the following limitations:

a. For each calendar year, the insured individual pays for
   the first $50 of reasonable charges. Expenses incurred
   in the last three months of a year may be credited
   toward the deductible for that year if the decuctible has
   not been previously met in that year and will also be
   credited toward the deductible for the following year.

b. After the deductible has been met, Medicare pays 80
   percent of the reasonable charges for covered services.

c. "Reasonable charges" are determined by the Medicare
   carriers, that is, hospitals and other health facilities, in
   each state and take into account the customary charges
   for medical and other health services in the community.

9. PREMIUMS—One-half of the premium for Part B
benefits is paid by the individual and one-half by the
government. The individual portion is paid monthly and, for
persons receiving social security or railroad retirement
benefits, is deducted from the monthly benefit check. Persons not entitled to retirement benefits but who have en-

rolled pay their premiums directly to the Social Security Administration. For the person who does not enroll during his initial enrollment period, but enrolls in a subsequent period, the monthly premium is increased by 10 percent of the monthly premium he would pay had he enrolled during his initial period, for each full 12 months in which he could have been, but was not, enrolled.

10. CLAIM PROCEDURE—Claims for payment under Part A are generally made by the hospital or extended care facility. Claims for payment under B are generally made by the physician or other person furnishing the service. Claims are made to the Medicare carrier in the locality where the services are furnished. If the physician does not accept responsibility for filing the claim for Part B benefits, the insured forwards the claim directly to the carrier for payment.

Mortgage

1. DEFINITIONS—A *mortgage* is an instrument in writing designating certain property, either real or personal, to secure the payment of a debt. When the debt is paid the mortgage becomes void and is released. The person who mortgages his property is called the *mortgagor*. The person to whom the mortgage is given is the *mortgagee*. Some states consider the mortgage as a conditional transfer of property, giving the mortgagee legal title until the debt and interest are paid; others regard the mortgagor as the holder of the legal title at all times and the mortgagee as the holder of an enforceable lien on the property.

2. GENERAL PRINCIPLES:

a. A mortgage may be made to cover future advances.

b. As the county records are public and may be examined by anyone, the injured party alone is responsible if he buys, or lends money on, a piece of property without first making certain that there are no encumbrances on it.

c. The law assumes that the mortgage contract covers all the agreements concerning the payment of the debt and the return of the property. The courts, therefore, ignore other agreements made at the same time. Later agreements, however, will hold if based on valid consideration.

d. Several mortgages may be made on the same piece of real estate. The one recorded first has the first lien.

e. A creditor cannot compel payment of the mortgage

before it is due. Neither can the debtor compel the creditor to accept the payment before it is due.

f. If after a foreclosure there is any deficit due the mortgagee, the mortgagor is still liable. See CHATTEL MORTGAGE.

g. A trust deed serves the same purpose as a real estate mortgage but conveys the property to a third party as trustee to hold title for the mortgagee, instead of conveying title directly to the mortgagee himself. This deed is very extensively used because it takes the place of a mortgage deed and renders the note negotiable. States frequently have statutory forms for trust deeds, and where such forms exist it is advisable to use them.

3. REQUIREMENTS—All real estate mortgages must be in writing, and under seal unless the seal has been abolished by statute. The instrument must clearly state the amount of the debt and the day on which it falls due. The property must be clearly described. The mortgage must then be acknowledged before the proper public official and properly recorded in the county records. The mortgagor usually gives a bond or note as evidence of the indebtedness, stating on its face that it is secured by a mortgage of the same date.

4. POSSESSION OF THE PROPERTY generally remains with the mortgagor. The mortgagor also receives all rents and profits from the property, and pays all taxes and other expenses.

5. IMPROVEMENTS TO THE PROPERTY—If a mortgagor erects buildings on mortgaged land and the mortgage is foreclosed, the mortgagee in taking possession gets all these additions. If the mortgagee erects buildings and the mortgagor thereafter redeems his land, he gets the buildings without paying for them.

6. ASSIGNMENT—A mortgagee can transfer, sell, or assign his mortgage at any time regardless of the wishes of the mortgagor. On the other hand, if the mortgagor wishes to sell his real estate he must sell subject to the mortgage. In other words, he can do nothing to invalidate the mortgagee's security.

7. INSURANCE—The property may be insured by both parties. In case of loss by fire the holder of the mortgage can collect the insurance that he had on the property. Practically all mortgages now contain provisions requiring the mortgagor to keep the property properly insured. The insurance policy contains a clause showing the name of the mortgagee or trustee and providing for his protection in case of loss by fire; the policy itself is usually held by the mortgagee.

8. FORECLOSURE—A *foreclosure* is a legal proceeding to sell the property mortgaged to satisfy the debt. If the property is sold to satisfy the debt, the mortgagor has a right to purchase it. The following steps are necessary for a foreclosure:

a. Application to a court.
b. A hearing by the court.
c. Referring to a master in chancery or a referee.
d. Advertising the property.
e. Public sale to the highest bidder.
f. Deeding the property to the purchaser.
g. Paying the money due to the mortgagee.
h. Returning any surplus to the mortgagor.

9. REDEMPTION—Formerly, a mortgagor could redeem his land only before or when the debt became due, but further time is now given. This right to redeem is called a *right in equity to redeem*, or an *equity of redemption*. The redemption period varies in different states according to statutes. This right to redeem is considered of so much importance that no party is permitted to lose it even by his own agreement. Even though the mortgagor agrees in the most positive terms to forfeit his equity of redemption, the law disregards such agreement and gives the debtor full time to redeem his property.

10. FORMS:

ASSIGNMENT OF MORTGAGE BY ENDORSEMENT

Know all men by these presents, That I, Henry Betzoid, the within named Mortgagee, for a consideration of Eight Hundred Dollars ($800), hereby sell, assign, transfer, and set over unto E. B. Newman, his heirs and assigns, the within named instrument of mortgage, and all the real estate, with appurtenances therein mentioned and described, and the promissory note, debts, and claims thereby secured, to have and to hold the same forever, subject to the conditions therein contained.

In witness whereof the party of the first part has hereunto set his hand and seal this third day of March, in the year of our Lord nineteen hundred and
. . . .

Sealed and delivered in the presence of
E. E. Hawthorne

(Most states no longer require this attestation.)

HENRY BETZOID   (Seal)

RELEASE

Know all men by these presents, That I, James Y.
Scammon, of the County of Cook, and State of Illinois,
for and in consideration of One Dollar ($1), to me in
hand paid, and for other good and valuable considerations, the receipt whereof is hereby confessed, do hereby grant, bargain, remise, convey, release, and quitclaim unto Samuel P. Smith and Sarah E. Smith, of
the County of Du Page and State of Illinois, all the
right, title, interest, claim, or demand whatsoever I
may have acquired in, through or by a certain indenture or mortgage deed, bearing date the first day of
January, A.D. 19 . . . ., and recorded in the recorder's
office of Du Page County, Illinois, in book 25 of
mortgages, page 100, in and to the premises situated
in the . . . . . . of . . . ., in said county of . . . . ., and in
said mortgage deed described as follows, to wit:
(description) and which said deed was made to secure
two certain promissory notes, bearing even date with
said deed, for the sum of Twenty-Five Hundred Dollars ($2,500).

Witness my hand and seal this 28th day of February, A.D. 19 . . . .

JAMES Y. SCAMMON   (Seal)

TRUST DEED

This deed, made this . . . . . day of . . . . ., 19 . . . ., between . . . . . of . . . . county of . . . . and state of
. . . . . of the one part, and . . . . of . . . ., and . . . . .
of . . . ., of the other part, witnesseth, that the party
of the first part doth grant unto the parties of the second part the following property, to wit:
[Insert description of property]
in trust, to secure to . . . . . . of . . . . ., in the state of
. . . . . ., the payment of . . . . dollars in . . . . . . years from
this date, with interest at . . . . percent per annum
thereon, according to a promissory note made by the

party of the first part to said .... for said sum.

In event that default shall be made in the payment of the above-mentioned sum as it becomes due and payable, then the trustees, or either of them, on being required so to do by ......, his executors, administrators, or assigns, shall sell the property hereby conveyed. And it is covenanted and agreed between the parties aforesaid that in case of a sale the same shall be made after first advertising the time, place, and terms thereof for ..... days in some newspaper published in the said county of ...., and upon the following terms, to wit: for cash as to so much of the proceeds as may be necessary to defray the expenses of executing this trust, the fees for drawing and recording this deed, if then unpaid, and to discharge the amount of money then payable upon said note; and if there be any residue of such purchase money, the same shall be made payable at such time, and be secured in such manner, as ....., his executors, administrators, or assigns, shall prescribe and direct, or in case of his or their failure to give such direction, at such time and in such manner as the trustees, or either of them, shall think fit. The party of the first part covenants to pay all taxes, assessments, dues, and charges upon the said property hereby conveyed so long as he or his heirs or assigns shall hold the same, and hereby waives the benefit of all homestead exemptions as to the debt secured by this deed.

If no default shall be made in the payment of the above-mentioned debt, then, upon the request of the party of the first part, a good and sufficient deed of release shall be executed to him at his own proper costs.

Witness, the hand .... and seal .... of said Grantor this ..... day of ...., A.D. 19 ......

.............(Seal)

.............(Seal)

Municipal Corporations

1. DEFINITION — A *municipal corporation* is a corporation formed to carry on the work of government in a town or city. Its charter is granted by the state and it possesses only such powers as the state confers upon it, and no others.

2. POWERS — A city government is usually given the

power:

a. To make its own laws or ordinances with reference to matters over which its charter gives it jurisdiction.

b. To enforce its laws.

c. To control all matters and things within its corporate boundaries within the limits fixed by its charter.

d. To issue bonds.

3. OFFICERS OF A MUNICIPAL CORPORATION—The mayor is usually the chief executive of a municipality, and the Board of Aldermen its lawmaking body. The titles of these officers vary widely, however, in the different states. Under the commission form of government the above offices are held by a commission of three or five men who have complete charge of the business of city government. The judicial power is usually vested in the police magistrate's court, or in larger cities in the municipal court. These are courts of limited jurisdiction only, however, and their jurisdiction does not supersede or conflict with that of the courts of the county in which they are situated.

4. WRONGFUL ACTS OF OFFICERS —The city is not responsible for damage for injuries to persons or property caused in the execution of a governmental duty. But what is considered a governmental duty is a question that has been the source of much litigation. The city is not liable for false arrest, false imprisonment, or assaults by police officers. If any wrongful act is committed by an officer while acting in his official capacity, he is liable personally.

5. THE CITY'S DUTY—It is the duty of the city government to provide and maintain safe and passable streets and highways, maintain police and fire protection, and provide for the general safety and welfare of its citizens.

6. LIABILITY—If the city fails to maintain safe and passable streets, the city is liable for damages resulting to those rightfully upon the streets, provided the city had notice that the streets were unsafe and impassable, and failed to exercise reasonable care to make the streets safe. It is almost universally held that a city is not liable for loss or injury resulting from failure to maintain proper police and fire protection.

7. POLICE POWER OF CITIES—The police power of a city extends to the city limits and a reasonable distance beyond the city limits in certain instances. The police magistrate, sometimes called the recorder, sits in a court having jurisdiction equal to that of a justice of the peace. The police magistrate and the police officers are bound to enforce the laws of the city, called *ordinances*. An officer may arrest a person:

a. When a wrongful act is committed in his presence.

b. Upon a valid warrant.

c. Upon *probable cause*.

An officer may not arrest on mere suspicion, but only upon a reasonable ground for belief in guilt by a reasonable, cautious, and prudent police officer judged in the light of his experience and training.

8.   SCHOOLS—The schools of a city are usually controlled by a board of education. This board has control and supervision over teachers, students, buildings, and all other matters pertaining to public education.

9.   PUBLIC SERVICE CORPORATIONS—Any corporation furnishing the public as a whole a service or commodity is called a *public service corporation*. Its activities are as a rule controlled and supervised by a public service commission having the power to fix prices and regulate many of the activities of the corporations that affect the public.

Negotiable Instruments

1.   DEFINITIONS—A *negotiable instrument* is any legal document that may be transferred by endorsement or delivery in such a way as to give the person receiving it the right to bring suit thereon in his own name. The person who promises to pay is called the *maker* or *drawer,* and the one to whom he promises is called the *payee*.

2.   KINDS OF NEGOTIABLE INSTRUMENTS—Almost every written contract or agreement to pay money is negotiable, in the sense that the owner can sell it to a third person who can enforce it against the maker. However, in the more strict sense of the word there are three common forms of negotiable paper, namely, checks, notes, and bills of exchange or drafts.

3.   FORM OF NEGOTIABLE INSTRUMENTS —The law does not require negotiable instruments to be in any prescribed form. However, certain things are necessary in all checks, notes, or bills of exchange to make them negotiable:

a.   The instrument must be in writing.

b.   It must be signed by the maker or drawer.

c.   It must contain a promise or order to pay.

d.   The promise or order must be unconditional.

e.   The promise or order must be a promise or order to pay a certain sum in money.

f.   The instrument must be payable on demand or at a fixed or determinable time in the future.

g.   The instrument must be payable to the order of some person, or to bearer.

h.   If the instrument is addressed to a drawee, as would be the case if it were a bill of exchange or draft, the drawee must be named or otherwise indicated in the instrument with reasonable certainty.

4. CONSIDERATION—While it is not always necessary to express any consideration in negotiable paper, it is safer to do so. When an instrument is in the hands of an innocent third party, the law assumes a valuable consideration. The words "for value received" usually appear on promissory notes.

5. PROTEST—A *protest* of a note, check, or draft is a formal statement by a notary public that the paper was presented for payment and was refused. The costs are added to the instrument. See also NOTARIES PUBLIC.

6. NEGOTIABILITY—The words "to bearer," or "to the order of," or words of like effect, render a paper negotiable. Any person capable of making a contract is capable of making a negotiable instrument. A person who receives a negotiable instrument under the conditions hereinafter mentioned becomes what is known as a "holder in due course," and certain defenses that might have been raised against the original holder cannot be raised against him. He must have taken the instrument under the following conditions:

a. The instrument must be complete and regular on its face.

b. It must not have been overdue, and the holder must not have known it was previously dishonored if such were the fact.

c. He must have taken it in good faith and paid value for it.

d. At the time he took it he must have had no notice of any infirmity in the instrument or defect in the title of the person negotiating it to him.

7. NOTES—A *note* is a simple written promise to pay a certain sum at a certain time to a person named therein. An *individual promissory note* is a note in which one party promises to pay another a certain sum of money at a specified time. A *joint promissory note* is the same as an individual note except that it is signed by two or more parties, all of whom are liable jointly but not severally. In a *joint and several promissory note* two or more parties severally and separately agree to pay a certain sum at a specified time, and each signer is responsible for the whole amount. Statutes in many states provide that all joint obligations shall be held to be joint and several.

8. TRANSFERRING NOTES—The following rules govern the

transferring of notes:

a. Instruments payable to bearer may be transferred by delivery, payable to order by endorsement.

b. An *endorser* is a person who writes his name on the back of a note or other instrument.

c. *Endorsement in blank* is an endorsement that does not mention the name of the person in whose favor it is made.

d. The endorser is liable for the payment of a note if the maker fails to meet it and the endorser is properly notified.

e. An endorser who is compelled to pay a note has a claim against the maker and against each endorser whose name appears above his own.

f. An endorser to whose order a note is drawn or endorsed can transfer it without becoming liable for its payment by writing the words "without recourse" over his signature on the back.

9. COLLECTING NOTES—The following rules govern the collection of notes:

a. A note destroyed by mistake or accident can be collected upon proof of loss.

b. Money paid by mistake must be refunded.

c. If no time is specified the note is payable on demand.

d. The *day of maturity* is the day on which a note becomes legally due.

e. In finding the day of maturity, actual days must be counted if the note falls due a specific number of days after the day on which it was drawn, but months are counted when the note falls due a specific number of months after the day on which it was drawn.

f. Negotiable paper to bearer or endorsed in blank, which has been lost or stolen, cannot be collected by the finder or thief, but a holder who innocently receives it in good faith before maturity for value received can hold it against the owner's claims.

g. A note made in one state, payable in another, must be governed by the laws of that state in which it is to be paid.

h. Demand for payment of a note must be made upon the day of maturity and at the place named. If no place is specified, it is payable at the maker's place of business or at his residence. In most of the states, when a note falls due on a Sunday or legal holiday, by statute the maker is given until the following day to pay the same.

i. An extension of the time of a note granted by the holder

releases sureties and endorsers, unless consent to such extension has been given by the endorsers or sureties.

j. If the maker refuses to pay a mature note presented to him by a holder in due course, the holder must immediately give notice of default to the endorser in order to hold that endorser liable for the debt.

10. PAYMENT OF NOTES—All the parties who have endorsed a note are liable for the full amount, but only one satisfaction can be recovered. In certain cases notes are unenforceable, especially when held by the original payee. Among such cases are the following:

a. A note given by one who is not of age, unless the minor ratified it after becoming of age.

b. A note made by an intoxicated person.

c. A note not witnessed, given by one who cannot write.

d. A note obtained by duress, by putting the maker in fear of illegal imprisonment, or by threats that would lead an ordinary person to fear injury to his person, his reputation, or his property.

e. A note obtained by fraud.

f. A note given for illegal consideration.

One who receives a note knowing it to have defects has no better right to collect it than the maker had to present it. If a person at the time of taking a note has notice that it is void because of fraud or for any other reason, he cannot collect it.

11. FORMS OF NOTES:

NEGOTIABLE BY ENDORSEMENT

$375.00   Naperville, Ill., Oct. 7, 19 . . . .
For value received, one year after date I promise to pay to the order of J. L. Nichols the sum of Three Hundred and Seventy-Five Dollars with interest at six percent from date until paid.

J. R. PRICE

NEGOTIABLE WITHOUT ENDORSEMENT

$100.00   Cleveland, O., Aug. 1, 19 ....
    Ninety days after date I promise to pay to bearer,
One Hundred Dollars, value received.

E. M. KECK

NOT NEGOTIABLE

$100.00   Chicago, Ill., Dec. 10, 19 ....
    Sixty days after date I promise to pay Geo. C. Dixon
One Hundred Dollars, value received.

EUGENE LANSING

A CORPORATION NOTE

$200.00   Augusta, Me., Mar. 18, 19 ....
    Nine months after date, the Granite Stone Compa-
ny, a corporation, promises to pay S. A. Chilton, or
order, Two Hundred Dollars, with interest at six percent. Value received.
Attest: I. K. Dawes, Secretary.

                    Granite Stone Company
                    O. R. PHILLIPS, President

Note.—If corporation notes are drawn and signed in the
above manner, the officers are not personally liable.

COLLATERAL NOTE

$500.00   Mendota, Tex., Sept. 25, 19 ....
    Sixty days after date, for value received, I promise
to pay to the order of T. J. Boyd, the sum of Five
Hundred Dollars, with interest at the rate of six percent per annum after date, having deposited United
States Bonds of the face value of Six Hundred Dollars
($600), which I authorize the holder of this Note, upon
the nonperformance of this promise at maturity, to
sell, at public or private sale, without further notice,
and to apply proceeds, or as much thereof as may be
necessary to the payment of this Note, and all neces-

sary expenses and charges, holding myself responsible
for any deficiency.

W. W. STRATTON

JUDGMENT NOTE

$2,000.00   Philadelphia, Pa., Jan. 4, 19 ...

Six months after date, for value received, I promise
to pay to the order of J. W. Krasley Two Thousand
Dollars, with interest at the rate of 6 percent per annum, after maturity, until paid.

And to secure the payment of said amount, I hereby
authorize any attorney of any court of record to appear for me in such court, in term time or vacation, at
any time after maturity, to waive a jury trial and con-
fess judgment, without process, in favor of the holder
of the note, for such amount as may appear to be paid
thereon, together with costs and five percent attorney's fees, and to waive and release all errors
which may intervene on any such proceedings, and
consent to immediate execution upon such judgment;
hereby ratifying and confirming all my said attorney
may do by virtue hereof.

GEORGE W. BAIRD

PAYABLE AT BANK

$440.00   Chicago, Ill., Oct. 10, 19 ...

Two years after date, for value received, I promise
to pay T. M. Culver, or order, Four Hundred Forty Dollars at Second National Bank, with interest at six percent per annum.

CHARLES HEARN

ON DEMAND

$25.67   Kansas City, Mo., Oct. 12, 19 ...

On demand I promise to pay to the order of J. T.
Connor, Twenty-Five 67-100 Dollars. Value received,
with interest at six percent.

A. H. SIMPSON

Note.—This note answers the same purpose as a note written one day after date.

JOINT NOTE

$200.00   Lisle, Ill., Jan. 1, 19 . . . .
    One year from date, we promise to pay D. F. Shaw, or order, Two Hundred Dollars. Value received. Interest at six percent.

J. LEWIS BEAN
B. A. WHITE

JOINT AND SEVERAL NOTE

$2,000.00   Ottawa, Ont., Nov. 25, 19 . . .
    Ten months after date, we, or either of us, promise to pay Maggie Patterson Two Thousand Dollars, value received. Interest at five percent.

J. C. HARDY
R. E. WOOD

PRINCIPAL AND SURETY NOTE

$600.00   New York, N.Y., Sept. 21, 19 . . . .
    For value received, on or before July 27, 19 . . . ., I promise to pay to the order of John Jackson, Six Hundred Dollars. Interest at five percent.

W. J. SHAW, Principal
THOS. RODDEN, Surety

Note.—The general form of a principal and surety note is for the principal to properly sign the note and for the surety to endorse it.

A NOTE BY ONE WHO CANNOT WRITE

$49.50   Cleveland, Ohio, Mar. 20, 19 . . .
    One year after date, I promise to pay N. Bowker, or order, Forty-Nine 50-100 Dollars, with interest at five percent. Value received.

H. A. STARR, Witness.

his
JOHN X ROURKE
mark

Note.—A note made by a person who cannot write should always be witnessed by a disinterested person.

MY OWN ORDER

$200.00   New Orleans, La., July 20, 19 ...
For value received, I promise to pay, sixty days after date, to my own order, Two Hundred Dollars, with interest at eight percent.

A. S. BARNARD

Note.— A note may be drawn to the maker's own order, with his endorsement in favor of the creditor.

NOTE SECURED BY A MORTGAGE

$1,000.00   Chicago, Ill., April 15, 19 ...
Six months after date I promise to pay to John Williams One Thousand Dollars with interest at six percent.
This note is secured by a mortgage of even date herewith from Robert Jones to John Williams.

ROBERT JONES

12. CHECKS—A *check* is an order drawn upon a bank, payable on demand. The person who writes the check is the *drawer;* the bank on which the check is drawn is called the *drawee;* the person to whom the check is made payable is called the *payee.*

13. SIGNATURE—A check must be properly signed by the drawer or his duly authorized agent. A signature made on behalf of the drawer by another person is valid if authorized. It should, of course, be written in ink, but a signature made with a pencil or rubber stamp is valid if intended as a signature.

14. PRESENTATION—A check must be presented for payment within a reasonable time after its issue, or the drawer will be discharged from liability thereon to the extent of the loss caused by the delay. It is generally held that one day after the receipt of the check is a reasonable time to present or forward the same for presentation.

15. THE AGREEMENT TO PAY is between the bank and the depositor. For this reason a check, of itself, does not operate as an assignment of any part of the funds to the credit of the drawer with the bank. Consequently, should the bank refuse to pay the check, the holder cannot bring action against the bank, unless or until the bank has accepted or certified the check. On the other hand, if the bank fails to fulfill its contract with the depositor, he has a just cause of action against the bank. Should the bank refuse to honor a

customer's check owing to an employee's mistake in book-keeping, the bank could be held responsible for any loss resulting therefrom.

16. CERTIFYING A CHECK — A certification of a check by the bank is equivalent to an acceptance, and discharges the drawer and all the endorsers preceding the holder who secures the certification. When a check is presented to a bank for this purpose, the bank charges the drawer's account with the amount so that, as far as the drawer and the bank are concerned, the check has actually been paid. Therefore, if a certified check is not presented at the drawer's bank for payment and is returned to the drawer, it should not be destroyed but should be redeposited as cash.

17. STOPPING PAYMENT — The drawer of the check may order the bank to stop payment on a check before it is presented. The bank is required to follow these instructions and is liable for any loss resulting from failure to do so.

18. FORGED CHECKS — The law insists that the banker exercise the greatest care in paying the checks of customers. If the signature has been forged or the amount of the check altered, the bank is liable for any improper payment. The drawer of the check must also use every precaution to prevent alterations. He should write in a way to avoid confusing the banker who is to pay the check. The bank is not responsible for any loss caused by negligence on the part of the drawer in making out the check.

19. VITAL POINTS ON CHECKS — A check is not due until presented. It is negotiable. It has no days of grace. Giving a check is not payment on an indebtedness, unless the check is paid, or unless it is accepted as payment. The death of the drawer of the check before it is presented to the bank renders the check null and void. The amount of the check should always be written out in words as well as in figures. If a raised check is paid by the bank, the bank can charge the depositor only the amount for which he drew the check, unless the raising of the check was made possible by the carelessness of the drawer. In that case the drawer would be responsible for the loss.

If you write a check for a stranger who needs identification at your bank, have him endorse the check in your presence and under his endorsement write "Endorsement above guaranteed," signing your name. He can then usually cash the check, without further identification, by signing his name again in the presence of the banker.

20. DRAFTS — A *draft* is a written order by one person on another for the payment of a specified sum of money to a designated third person. The one who writes the draft is called the *drawer*, the one on whom it is written, the *drawee*,

and the one to whom it is to be paid, the *payee*.

21. KINDS OF DRAFTS—Drafts may be made payable at sight, on demand, at a certain time after date, or after sight. A *sight draft* or *demand draft* is drawn by one person on another and is payable when presented. *Time drafts* are similar to sight drafts, but are payable a certain number of days after presentation. A *bill of exchange* is an unconditional order in writing addressed by one person to another, signed by the person giving it, requiring the person to whom it is addressed to pay on demand or at a fixed or determinable future time a certain sum of money to order or to bearer. The term includes drafts and checks.

22. ACCEPTANCE—Sight and demand drafts are presented for payment only. Time drafts require acceptance by the party against whom they are drawn in order to bind him. The usual method of acceptance is to write across the face of the draft in red ink the word "accepted," followed by the date and the signature of the drawee. Should the person on whom the draft is drawn die before it was accepted, it should be presented to his legal representative for acceptance. When either acceptance or payment is refused, the draft may be protested like any note or check. Drafts are negotiable both before and after acceptance.

23. FORMS OF DRAFTS:

BANK DRAFT

$100.00 State of Illinois, May 10, 19 ....
The First National Bank of Naperville. Pay to the order of F. A. Lueben, One Hundred Dollars.
To Union National Bank, W. L. HETZ, Cashier
Chicago, Ill.

DEMAND DRAFT

$100.00 Troy Grove, Ill., Aug. 1, 19 ....
On demand pay to the order of Frank Myers at the Mendota First National Bank, One Hundred Dollars. Value received.
To Charles Lerch, A. S. HUDSON
Mendota, Ill.

SIGHT DRAFT

$500.00 Naperville, Tenn., July 10, 19 ....
At sight pay to the order of C. Parman, Five Hundred Dollars, and charge to the account of
To Jessee Lerch, H. H. ZEMMER
Meriden, Ill.

TIME DRAFT

$450.30   Ottawa, Fla., July 5, 19 . . . .
    Ten days from date pay to J. L. Nichols, or order,
Four Hundred Fifty 30-100 Dollars. Value received.
To Alvin Brown,   C. E. LAMALE
    Ottawa, Fla.

24.   ENDORSEMENTS—An *endorsement* is a writing on the
back of a negotiable instrument for the purpose of transferring the title or ownership from one person to another. The
writing may be in pen or pencil upon any part of the instrument or upon a paper attached thereto. It consists ordinarily
of the payee's signature and those of other holders, if any.
25.   HOW TO ENDORSE—Write across the back of the
paper, not lengthwise, near the left end. Always endorse a
check or note exactly as your name appears on the face. If
the check is payable to F. Black, do not write Frank Black.
If your name is misspelled, endorse first as it appears on the
face and then write your correct signature underneath. No
written explanation is necessary: banks are familiar with
this practice. The same rules govern the endorsement of
notes, drafts, and other written instruments. A check or
other instrument may be endorsed and title thereby
transferred many times. Each endorser is liable to those
who endorse after him.
26.   KINDS OF ENDORSEMENTS—An *endorsement in blank*
is made when the payee simply signs his name in the proper
place, across the left end of the reverse side, without any
statement of conditions. Such a note or check is negotiable
without further endorsement. Endorsement in blank is commonly used when a check is deposited or cashed at a bank. It
should not be used when there is danger of the check's being
lost or stolen.
    An *endorsement in full* or special endorsement consists of
writing the name of the person to whom, or to whose order,
the money is to be paid, followed by the payee's signature.
For example: "Pay to F. Black or order, J. Jones"; when endorsed in this form, the check cannot be cashed until F.
Black endorses it.
    In a *qualified endorsement* the endorser relieves himself
of any liability in connection with the instrument, by writing above his signature the words "Without recourse"; thus,
"Without recourse, J. Jones."
    A *restrictive endorsement* limits the payment of the note,
bill, or check. The endorser writes "pay to F. Black only," or
"for deposit in the First National Bank," signing his name
underneath. A check or other instrument so endorsed cannot be further negotiated by the person or bank receiving it.

Restrictive endorsement is a wise precaution when there is danger of a negotiable instrument being lost or stolen after endorsement.

A *conditional endorsement* is one directing payment only upon the performance of a certain condition. The endorser's liability is thereby limited. For example, "Pay to the order of F. Black unless he previously receives the amount from my agent, J. Jones." Neither the original character of the note nor its negotiability is affected by such an endorsement. It may affect, however, the title of the one to whom it is transferred.

Endorsement by an agent is made in the following form: "J. Jones, by H. Smith, his agent." In this manner the agent endorses for his principal.

In a *guaranteed endorsement* one party guarantees payment on a note for another party. He writes above his signature "I hereby guarantee payment of this note," or words to like effect. He is then absolutely liable for the amount due by the terms of the note in case the maker fails to pay. In effect, he becomes a co-maker.

27. IOU—An *IOU* is not a promissory note, and is not negotiable. It is evidence of a debt due by virtue of a previous contract. The following is an example:

Chicago, Ill., June 4, 1940

Mr. A. O. Rogers
   IOU Sixty Dollars ($60.00).

W. G. ALLEN

28. DUE BILLS—A *due bill* is not payable to order, nor is it assignable by mere endorsement. It is simply the acknowledgment of a debt, yet it may be transferred. It may be payable in money, in merchandise, or in services.

Due bills do not draw interest unless so specified. Common forms are the following:

$125.00   Chicago, Aug. 14, 19 ....
   Due Henry Harrington, for value received, One Hundred and Twenty-Five Dollars with interest at six percent.

Q. YINZER

ON DEMAND

$250.00   Naperville, Ill., July 1, 19 . . . . .

Due E. E. Miller, on demand, Two Hundred Fifty Dollars in goods from my store, for value received.

A. T. HANSON

IN MERCHANDISE

$1,000.00   Lincoln, Neb., Nov. 1, 19 . . . .

Due R. William, One Thousand Dollars, payable in wheat at market price, on the first day of January, 19 . . . . . .

CHARLES SCHUERER

29. RECEIPTS—A *receipt* is an acknowledgment in writing that a certain sum of money or a thing has been received by the party giving and signing the same. A complete receipt requires the following statements: (a) that a payment has been received; (b) the date of the payment; (c) the amount of article received; (d) from whom received, and, if for another, on whose behalf payment is made; (e) to what debt or purpose it is to be applied; (f) the signature of the person receiving the property, and, if for another, on whose behalf it was received.

30. GENERAL PRINCIPLES GOVERNING RECEIPTS—When an agent signs a receipt, he should sign his principal's name and then write his name underneath as agent. If payment is made upon account, upon a special debt, or in full, it should be so stated in the receipt. It is not necessary to take a receipt on paying a note, draft, or other instrument endorsed by the payee, because the instrument itself becomes a receipt. If a receipt is obtained through fraud, or given under error or mistake, it is void. If the giving and taking of receipts were more generally practiced in business transactions, less trouble, fewer lawsuits, and the saving of thousands of dollars would result.

31. FORMS OF RECEIPTS:

RECEIPT FOR PAYMENT ON ACCOUNT

$250.00   Naperville, Ill., July 6, 19 . . . .

Received of J. L. Nichols, Two Hundred and Fifty Dollars on account.

J. K. ROHMER

RECEIPT FOR SETTLEMENT OF AN ACCOUNT

$220.14   Joliet, Ill., March 20, 19 ....
     Received of Thomas Rourke, Two Hundred and
Twenty 14-100 Dollars, in full settlement of account
to date.

C. S. SELBY

RECEIPT IN FULL OF ALL DEMANDS

$1,000.00   Meriden, Conn., Jan. 14, 19 ....
     Received of C. F. Hetche, One Thousand Dollars, in
full of all demands to date.

O. N. OBRIGHT

RECEIPT FOR A PARTICULAR BILL

$400.00   Brooklyn, N. Y., Aug. 1, 19 ....
     Received of Morris Cliggitt, Four Hundred Dollars,
in payment for a bill of Merchandise.

R. ZACHMAN

RECEIPT FOR RENT

$40.00   Snyder, Tex., Mar. 20, 19 ....
     Received of L. Heininger, Forty Dollars in full for
one month's rent, for month ending April 20, 19 .....,
for resident at 44 Olive Street.

J. LEWIS BEAN

RECEIPT FOR A NOTE

$1,220.00
     Received, Buffalo, March 6, 19 ...., from Messrs.
Taylor & Co., their note of this date, at three months,
our favor, for Twelve Hundred and Twenty Dollars;
which, when paid, will be in full of account rendered
to 1st instant.

C. H. OLIVER

RECEIPT FOR SERVICES

$44.00   Lemont, Ill., July 23, 19 ....
     Received of Samuel Lynn, Forty-Four Dollars, in
full for services to date.

DANIEL FURBUSH

RECEIPT FOR MONEY ADVANCED ON A CONTRACT

$500.00   Chicago, Ill., May 10, 19 . . . .

Received of Arthur Kahl the sum of Five Hundred
Dollars, part payment on contract to build for him a
house at No. 1439 Perry St., Chicago.

CARL DIENST

RECEIPT FOR INTEREST DUE ON A MORTGAGE

$75.00   Chicago, August 1, 19 . . . .

Received of G. A. Caton, Seventy-Five Dollars in full
of six months' interest due this day, on his note to me
dated August 1st, 19 . . . . ., for Twenty-Five Hundred
Dollars ($2,500), secured by mortgage on property at
1430 Maple Street, Chicago.

EDWARD TRONT

Notaries Public

1. DEFINITION—A *notary public* is a state officer whose
functions are (a) to attest and certify, by his hand and official seal, various documents, in order to give them authenticity in other jurisdictions, (b) to take acknowledgments of
deeds and other conveyances and instruments, and to certify the same, and (c) to perform other official acts, the power
to do which is conferred by statutory enactment As a
general rule the functions of a notary are ministerial, not
judicial. They are confined to the civil, as distinguished
from the criminal, branch of the law.

2. THE OFFICE AND ITS FUNCTIONS—The office of notary
public as it exists in the several states today is the out-
growth of various practices traceable to the Roman Empire.
Merely a scribe in ancient times, the notary has been
granted increasing power and more duties by successive legislative enactments in order to meet the needs of changing
conditions and a growing civilization. His commission is
granted upon representation of his capacity and integrity.
In accepting office the notary contracts the obligation to fill
it intelligently and honestly. A notary public is responsible
for a number of important functions.

3. PROTESTING BILLS OF EXCHANGE —A notary public is
empowered to protest inland and foreign bills of exchange
and promissory notes, authenticating their dishonor by the
refusal of the drawee or payee to accept or pay them on
presentation or when due. The term *protest* as applied to

commercial paper means the taking of such steps as are required to charge or fix liability upon one secondarily liable, such as an endorser. As applied to the notarial act, it means a declaration made in writing by a notary public after doing the acts certified, that the bill or note to which it relates was, on the day it became due, presented for payment, and that payment was refused.

4. AUTHENTICATION OF DOCUMENTS—A notary public is empowered to authenticate transfers or conveyances of property, and other documents required by law to be authenticated. To *authenticate* a document means for a notary to certify under his hand and seal of office, together with a notice of the date and, in most states, the expiration date of his commission, such facts as the law requires to give the document operative effect.

5. TAKING DEPOSITIONS—A notary may take depositions under the rules and instructions of the courts when cases are pending. A *deposition* is the testimony of a witness taken down in writing, under oath or affirmation before a notary public, and usually subscribed by the witness, pursuant to special authority granted by a court after notice to the adverse party. It is authenticated by the notary.

6. TAKING ACKNOWLEDGMENTS—A notary public may take acknowledgments of various written instruments. An *acknowledgment* is an oral declaration or admission made by one who has executed a document, made before a notary public or other officer authorized by law to take acknowledgments, to the effect that the execution is his act and deed. The written certificate on the document endorsed by the officer taking the acknowledgment, certifying to the facts of the same, is sometimes referred to as "an acknowledgment," but is more properly called a *certificate of acknowledgment*. It is not part of the execution of a document, but only evidence of execution. The function of a certificate of acknowledgment is twofold—to authorize the document to be given in evidence without further proof of its execution, and to entitle it to be recorded. At least six essential facts must appear in a certificate of acknowledgment: (a) the designation of the officer making the certificate; (b) the name of the person making the acknowledgment, and that he or she personally appeared before the officer; (c) that there was an acknowledgment; (d) that the person who made the acknowledgment was identified as the one who executed the instrument; (e) that such identity was personally known or proved by the officer taking the acknowledgment; and (f) the day and year when the acknowledgment was made.

7. TAKING AFFIDAVITS—A notary public may take affidavits as to the truth of statements made in legal papers for use in proceedings before courts of civil or maritime jurisdiction. An *affidavit* is a voluntary statement, formally reduced to writing and sworn to or affirmed and subscribed before a notary public. See AFFIDAVITS.

8. ADMINISTERING OATHS—A notary may administer oaths and affirmations as to correctness of accounts. An *oath* is an outward pledge, given by the person taking it, that his attestation or promise is made under an immediate sense of his responsibility to God.

9. FORM AND MANNER OF ADMINISTERING OATHS, AFFIDAVITS, AND AFFIRMATIONS—The customary and approved manner of administering an oath or taking an affidavit is to have the person making the same raise his hand and swear by the ever-living God. There should be at least some manifestation that the officer and the person taking the oath understand the nature of their undertaking; a mere mental process is not sufficient. In many states the form and manner of taking an oath are prescribed by law.

Any person who desires may in lieu of an oath or affidavit take and subscribe or assent to an affirmation, which is administered by the officer repeating the words, "You do solemnly, sincerely and truly declare and affirm that," etc., "and so you do affirm." It is not unusual to ask the question, "Do you swear or affirm" rather than to wait for the deponent to express his desire. A strict and solemn compliance with these forms is important. Any person who willfully and falsely swears or affirms to any material matter is guilty of perjury. The average citizen is inclined to attach only such importance and solemnity to these acts as the officer administering them shows. To perform these acts in a perfunctory manner is to deprive them of their intended value, and in some instances to encourage perjury.

FORM OF AFFIDAVIT OR AFFIRMATION

STATE OF PENNSYLVANIA,)
COUNTY OF PHILADELPHIA.) ss.

Allen B. White, being duly sworn (or affirmed), according to law, deposes and says (or in case of affirmation, in lieu of "deposes and says" insert "affirms and declares") that he is the person who executed the foregoing instrument (or if by an officer or agent of a corporation, insert in lieu of "he is the person," etc., the following: "he is the |name of office| of the |name of corporation| above named, that he has authority

LAW FOR EVERYONE 121

from it to make this affidavit [or affirmation] in its behalf); and that the facts therein set forth are true to the best of his (add "and its" where made by officer or agent for corporation) knowledge, information and belief.

Sworn (or affirmed) and
subscribed before me this
22nd day of November, A.D. 19 ....

ALLEN B. WHITE
C. D. BLACK

(Seal)
Stamp com. expires.

**FORM OF ACKNOWLEDGMENT RECOMMENDED BY
AMERICAN BAR ASSOCIATION—
BY SINGLE PERSON OR BY HUSBAND AND WIFE**

STATE OF ILLINOIS,)
COUNTY OF COOK.) ss.

On this .... day of ...., 19 ....., before me, the subscriber (here insert title of officer), personally appeared A. B. (and C. B., his wife, if so), to me known to be the person (or persons) described in and who executed the foregoing instrument, and acknowledged that he (she or they) executed the same as his (her or their) free act and deed.
(Seal)

(Signature and title), etc.

Parent and Child

1. ANCIENT AUTHORITY—In past ages the father was by custom considered an absolute monarch of the home. In the Oriental countries of today the same custom still prevails. Modern progress and modern ideas, however, have changed old customs, and the authority of the parent in Western countries has been considerably limited by law.

2. RIGHTS OF PARENTS—The parent has the right of control over his child, and has all reasonable authority to enforce obedience. As long as the parent treats his child properly, no one has a right to interfere with his authority, or take the child away and retain him against the wishes of the parent.

3. A RUNAWAY CHILD—A child has no right to leave home without permission of the parent, and should a child run away he can be brought back by force. If relatives or other parties keep him and refuse to give him up, the parent

by legal process can obtain possession of his child, unless it can be shown that the parent is brutal, or is not a fit person, on account of drunkenness or other causes, to take proper care of the child.

4. PUNISHMENT OF CHILDREN—A parent has a right to punish his minor child, provided he is not guilty of cruelty or brutality, which are crimes punishable by severe legal penalties. The parent must be reasonable in his punishment, and in no way injure the health of the child.

5. RIGHTS TO EARNINGS—A parent is entitled to all the earnings of his minor child. If the child should refuse to turn over his earnings to the parent, the employer of the child may be notified, and be compelled to pay the parent only.

6. SPECIAL RIGHTS—The parent may, however, free his child from all obligations to himself and allow the child to collect his own wages for himself. When a parent thus makes public such a declaration, he cannot thereafter collect the child's wages.

7. THE PROPERTY OF THE CHILD—A parent may control the earnings of the child, yet he has no control of the property belonging to the child, acquired by gift, by legacy, or in any other way. If a parent should appropriate his child's property, it would be just as criminal in the eyes of the law as stealing.

8. PARENT'S OBLIGATION TO SUPPORT—Parents are legally held for the support of their minor children. The fact that a child has property does not relieve the parent from the support of his child; he can, however, apply to court and get permission to use part, or all of the income of the property for the child's support.

9. ILLEGITIMATE CHILDREN—It is a parent's duty to support an illegitimate child. Such a child has legally no father, but his *putative father,* as he is called, may be compelled to furnish the child with reasonable support so that it shall not become a burden upon the community. All children born in wedlock are legitimate, unless it is proved that the husband could not possibly be the father. The adultery of the wife cannot affect the legitimacy of the child. It is presumed to be that of the husband. It makes no difference how soon after marriage the child is born. A child born the same day as the marriage, if birth is subsequent to the ceremony, is legitimate unless there is reason for believing that the husband is not the actual father.

10. EFFECT OF ILLEGITIMACY —The only important legal effect of illegitimacy is that the child usually cannot inherit property from his father. He may, of course, take a legacy given to him by his putative father's will, but if there is no will he generally cannot inherit. An illegitimate child

usually inherits from his mother even though there are legitimate children.

11. CHILDREN'S OBLIGATIONS—Where the parents or grandparents are unable to support themselves, in many states the child is legally held for their support and care.

12. CRIMES—A parent cannot be held for crimes committed by his minor child. If a child commits a premeditated crime, he is personally liable.

13. GUARDIAN—If a child has no parents living, a guardian may be appointed. If the child has arrived at a certain age, varying in different states, he may petition the court for the appointment of his own guardian, who will in a legal sense exercise the prerogatives of a parent.

14. CONTRACTS WITH A MINOR—A contract made by a minor is valid if it is for necessities. Just what constitutes a necessity depends on the circumstances and is a matter for the jury to decide. If a minor contracts for other things, the contract is not always void, but may be avoided by the minor. Even though a minor fraudulently represents himself to be of age and makes a contract for goods, the seller cannot recover on the contract. His only remedy is an action of deceit. A minor who has a parent or guardian cannot make a contract even for necessities. But if the minor receives and retains such articles, with the permission of the parent or guardian, the parent or guardian will be deemed to have ratified the contract and will be held personally liable. If the parent or guardian is unwilling to provide the necessities he can be compelled to do so by the courts.

Parliamentary Law

1. NECESSITY FOR PARLIAMENTARY RULES—In every community it is necessary to hold public meetings from time to time. In order to expedite the proceedings of such meetings, as well as to settle matters of dispute, it is necessary that rules of procedure be adopted. In order to be able to take an intelligent interest and to participate in such meetings, it is essential that young and old be informed of the most important points of parliamentary rules.

2. RULES OF PARLIAMENTARY LAW—The following rules and suggestions will be found helpful in conducting public meetings:

a. The chairman selected should be a person of maturity and one held in respect and confidence.

b. Permission to address the meeting must be obtained

from the chairman by rising and saying: "Mr. President" or "Mr. Chairman."

c. No speaker should be interrupted unless his remarks are out of order, when he should be called to order by the chair. If the chairman fails to call him to order, any member may do so.

d. The proper way to make a motion is to say: "Mr. Chairman, I move that (here state motion)."

e. When a motion is presented to the meeting and seconded, it should be stated or read by the secretary or chairman.

f. After debate, the motion should be put to the meeting, the chairman announcing the result.

g. A speaker is out of order when he is speaking of matters and things foreign to the issue before the house.

h. Any violation of rules must be recognized and checked by the presiding officer.

i. When a member is called to order by the president, he should take his seat, unless he is permitted to explain.

j. Any ruling of the chairman may be appealed and decided by a vote.

k. It is the privilege of any member to call for the yeas and nays and thus put on record the vote of every member.

l. The chairman is the servant, not the master, of the house. To get rid of an undesirable chairman, the house may refuse to do any business, or may adjourn.

m. A motion to adjourn is always in order and is not debatable.

3. RULES OF ORDER—Common problems of parliamentary order are listed below. Following each item is a group of numbers which refer to the numbered points of order in section 4. Simply look up each of these references to learn what points of order apply to each specific problem.

Forms in which questions
   may be put 28, 29, 30, 31, 32
Questions of precedence
   of questions 19, 20, 21, 22, 23, 24, 25, 26, 27
Motion to withdraw a
   motion 1, 5, 7, 9, 13, 14, 16
To take up a question
   out of its proper order . . .   1, 5, 7, 9, 12, 14, 16
Motion to take from the
   table 1, 5, 7, 11, 12, 14, 16
Motion to suspend the
   rules 3, 5, 8, 10, 13, 14, 16

To substitute in the na-
ture of an amend-
ment.................... 3, 5, 8, 9, 13, 14, 16

Motion to make subject
a special order.......... 3, 5, 8, 9, 12, 14, 16

Question whether subject
shall be discussed....... 1, 5, 7, 9, 12, 15, 17

Motion that committee
do not rise.............. 1, 5, 7, 10, 13, 14, 16

Motion to refer a ques-
tion..................... 3, 6, 8, 10, 13, 14, 16

Motion to reconsider an
undebatable question.... 1, 5, 7, 10, 13, 14, 18

Motion to reconsider a
debatable question...... 3, 6, 7, 10, 13, 14, 16

Reading papers........... 1, 5, 7, 9, 13, 14, 16

Questions of privilege..... 3, 5, 8, 9, 13, 14, 16

Questions touching pri-
ority of business........ 1, 5, 8, 9, 13, 14, 16

Motion for previous
question................ 1, 5, 7, 9, 13, 14, 16

Motion to postpone in-
definitely............... 3, 6, 7, 9, 13, 14, 16

Motion to postpone to a
definite time............ 4, 5, 8, 9, 13, 14, 16

Motion for the orders of
the day................. 1, 5, 7, 9, 13, 15, 17

Objection to considera-
tion of question......... 1, 5, 7, 9, 12, 15, 17

Motion to limit debate
on question............. 1, 5, 8, 9, 12, 14, 16

Motion to lay on the
table................... 1, 5, 7, 11, 13, 14, 16

Leave to continue speaking
after indecorum......... 1, 5, 7, 9, 13, 14, 16

Motion to extend limits
of debate on question.... 1, 5, 8, 9, 13, 14, 16

Motion to commit......... 3, 6, 8, 9, 13, 14, 16

Motion to close debate
on question............. 1, 5, 8, 9, 12, 14, 16

Call to order............. 1, 5, 7, 9, 13, 15, 17

**Motion to appeal from
Speaker's decision
generally**............... 3, 5, 7, 9, 13, 14, 17

**Motion to appeal from
Speaker's decision
re indecorum**........... 1, 5, 8, 9, 13, 14, 17

Motion to amend the

4. POINTS OF ORDER:

1. Question undebatable; sometimes remarks tacitly allowed.
2. Undebatable if another question is before the assembly.
3. Debatable question.
4. Limited debate only on propriety of postponement.
5. Does not allow reference to main question.
6. Opens the main question to debate.
7. Cannot be amended.
8. May be amended.
9. Can be reconsidered.
10. Cannot be reconsidered.
11. An affirmative vote on this question cannotsbe reconsidered.
12. Requires two-thirds vote, unless special rules have been enacted.
13. Simple majority suffices to determine the question.
14. Motion must be seconded.
15. Does not require to be seconded.
16. Not in order when another has the floor.
17. Always in order though another may have the floor.
18. May be moved and entered on the record when another has the floor, but the business then before the assembly may not be put aside. The motion must be made by one who voted with the prevailing side, and on the same day the original vote was taken.
19. Fixing the time to which an adjournment may be made; ranks first.
20. To adjourn without limitation; second.
21. Motion for the Orders of the Day; third.
22. Motion to lay on the table; fourth.
23. Motion for the previous question; fifth.
24. Motion to postpone definitely; sixth.
25. Motion to commit; seventh.
26. Motion to amend; eighth.
27. Motion to postpone indefinitely; ninth.
28. On motion to strike out words ("Shall the words stand as part of the motion?") unless a majority sustains the words they are struck out.

29. On motion for previous question the form to be observed is: "Shall the main question be now put?" This, if carried, ends debate.

30. On an appeal from the chair's decision ("Shall the decision be sustained as the ruling of the house?") the chair is usually sustained.

31. A motion for Orders of the Day is put in the following form: "Will the house now proceed to the Orders of the Day?" This, if carried, supersedes intervening motions.

32. When an objection is raised to considering question ("Shall the question be considered?") objection may be made by any member before debate has commenced, but not subsequently.

Partnership

1. DEFINITION—The Uniform Partnership Act defines a *partnership* as "an association of two or more persons to carry on as coowners a business for profit."

2. KINDS OF PARTNERSHIP—A *general partnership* is one in which the partners agree to enter into a certain business without limitation or condition. There may also be a partnership in a single transaction, such as to buy or sell a single oil lease. An *implied partnership* is one in which one party acts in such a way as to lead outsiders to believe that partnership actually exists. In a *special* or *limited partnership* there may be general partners with unlimited liability and special partners with limited liability.

3. KINDS OF PARTNER—A *general partner* is one who is generally known as a partner and whose liability is not limited. A *secret partner* is one who is not openly declared as a partner. A *silent partner* takes no active part in the business but shares in the profits, losses, and liabilities. A *nominal partner* is held out as a partner without sharing in the profits or losses of the business, although he may be active in it.

4. FORMING A PARTNERSHIP—A partnership is formed by an agreement, usually in writing, though it may be oral. Any persons competent to transact business in their own names may become partners. Partners often have separate fields of endeavor, each doing the work for which he is best fitted. The article of agreement should specify the division of profits and losses and should be very carefully drawn. In the absence of any written agreement the law assumes that the partners share profits and losses equally. A partnership may hold both real and personal property.

5. LIABILITY — Each partner is a general agent and has full authority to act for the partnership. Not only common property, but also all the private property of each partner may be taken to satisfy the debts of the firm. A partner cannot make the firm responsible for his separate or private debts, nor bind the firm by entering into engagements unconnected with, or foreign to, the partnership. The authority of a partner usually extends to the making or endorsing of negotiable paper, and to all transactions fairly connected with the business. A person who, after due care, lends money to one member of a partnership firm for the firm, can hold the firm liable even if the money is fraudulently appropriated by the partner to his own use. An illegal contract made by one partner will not bind the partnership.

6. HOW TO AVOID LIABILITY — In order to avoid individual liability in transacting business, the partners may form a corporation or a limited liability partnership. The latter consists of two or more general partners and also special partners, whose contribution and liability are made known to the public. These special partners are liable only for the amount of capital they advanced.

7. DISSOLUTION — There are numerous ways in which a partnership may be dissolved:

a. Any partner, upon due notice to the others, may withdraw at any time provided no specific date for the dissolution of the partnership is mentioned in the articles of agreement. There is some authority, however, to the effect that the power to withdraw should be exercised in good faith so as not to prejudice the other partners. The retiring partner should notify the public of his retirement in order to relieve himself from future liability.

b. The partnership may be dissolved by mutual consent.

c. The death of one of the partners automatically dissolves the partnership.

d. The taking in of a new partner constitutes a new partnership. This is usually a matter of reorganization, and the new partnership may or may not assume liabilities of the old firm.

e. The insanity or bankruptcy of one of the partners ends the partnership.

f. A court may dissolve a partnership for any good reason such as incapacity, drunkenness, or fraud.

g. The expiration of the time specified in the articles of partnership acts as a dissolution.

8. LIQUIDATION — In case of failure, the assets of the partnership must be used to pay the debts of the partner-

ship, the assets of the partners to pay their personal debts. If in either case any property remains, the partnership property is applied on the personal debts, and the partners' personal property must go towards the partnership debts. The affairs of the insolvent partnership are usually placed in the hands of one of the partners, subject to control of the court, or turned over to a receiver appointed by the court, either of whom has the right to liquidate the affairs of the partnership.

9. FORMS:

ARTICLES OF COPARTNERSHIP

Articles of agreement, made . . . . ., 19 . . . . ., between . . . . . . and . . . .

The said parties hereby agree to become copartners, under the firm name of . . . . . ., and as such partners to carry on together the business of buying and selling all sorts of dry goods, at . . . . . . street, in the city of . . . .

The said . . . . agrees to contribute Two Thousand Dollars ($2,000) to the capital of said firm; and the said . . . . . agrees to contribute One Thousand Dollars ($1,000) to the same; the sum of Twenty-Five Hundred Dollars ($2,500) of said capital to be expended in the purchase of a stock in trade.

The said . . . . . shall have exclusive charge of all the buying for the firm.

All the net profits arising out of the business shall be divided in the following proportions, two-thirds to the said . . . . . and one-third to the said . . . .

Each partner shall devote all his time, attention, and efforts to the said business.

Neither partner shall, without the consent of the other in writing, sign any bond, bill or note as surety, or otherwise become obligated as security for any other person.

Witness the hands and seals of the parties hereto, this . . . day of . . . . , A.D. 19 . . . .

. . . . (Seal)
. . . . (Seal)

AGREEMENT TO DISSOLVE PARTNERSHIP

We, the undersigned, do mutually agree that the within mentioned partnership be, and the same is, hereby dissolved, except for the purpose of final liquidation and settlement of the business thereof, and

upon such settlement wholly to cease and determine.
Witness our hands and seals this ...... day of
....., nineteen hundred and .....
Signed, Sealed and Delivered
in Presence of

....

....

(Most states do not require this attestation.)

.... (Seal)

Passports

1. DEFINITIONS—A *passport* is a warrant of authority to
travel, granted by a government to a citizen intending to
travel outside the country. Passports are issued by the
United States Department of State for the purpose of providing citizens and nationals who are traveling abroad with
documentary evidence identifying them as entitled to the
protection afforded such persons. Some countries require a
visa, that is, a stamp of approval, to be affixed to the
passport by the consulate of the country to be visited. Other
countries do not insist on this formality. Some countries
that do not require visas ask visitors making a short stay to
fill out tourist cards.

The United States government does not issue passports
for travel to Communist-controlled parts of China, Korea, or
Vietnam or to Albania or Cuba unless special circumstances
prevail that require travel to either Albania or Cuba.

2. APPLICATION—An application for a passport must be
executed before a clerk of a federal court or a state court
authorized to accept applications, in some post offices in
metropolitan areas, or before an agent of the Passport Office, Department of State. Passport agents are located in
Boston, Chicago, Honolulu, Los Angeles, Miami, New
Orleans, New York, San Francisco, Seattle, and Washington, D.C.

3. OBTAINING A PASSPORT—To obtain a passport, a na-
tive-born citizen must submit a birth certificate, baptismal
certificate, or a certified copy of the record of baptism. If
these are not available, he may submit secondary evidence.
No witness is required if proof of identity is sufficient.
Otherwise a witness must take oath that he has known the
applicant for over two years. A person claiming U.S. citizenship through birth abroad must present a consular report of
birth, birth certificate, certificate of citizenship, or evidence
of parent's citizenship. A person who claims American
citizenship by naturalization must submit with his application a certificate of naturalization. A person who claims
citizenship by the naturalization of a parent must submit

with his application for passport the naturalization certificate of the parent. Persons traveling because of a contract with the U.S. government must submit letters from their employer stating their position and the purpose of travel. Persons of military draft age may receive passports but should inform their draft boards of their whereabouts. An alien leaving the United States must request passport facilities from his home government. He must have a permit from his local Collector of Internal Revenue. If he wishes to return to the United States, he should request a re-entry permit from the Immigration and Naturalization Service before he departs.

4. PHOTOGRAPHS—Two recently taken photographs (duplicates) of each person named in the application must be submitted. One photograph should be affixed to the application; the other, signed by the applicant, must accompany the application unattached. A group photograph should be used when a wife, or wife and children, are included in one application. Photographs must be full face, on thin paper, with a light background, and not over 3 x 3 inches nor less than 2½ x 2½ inches in size. Photographs printed on photographic paper the back of which is glazed will not adhere to passports and therefore will not be accepted.

5. HEALTH REQUIREMENTS—A valid smallpox vaccination certificate issued within three years must be shown by all persons entering the United States. Valid vaccination certificates are required if a person has left a cholera-infected area within the last five days. Similar certificates are required from persons who left yellow fever-infected areas within six days and who are destined for receptive areas in the United States. Vaccinations should be recorded on International Certificates of Vaccination. The smallpox and cholera vaccination certificates should be stamped by the local or state health office.

6. FEES—Passport fees are established by Congress. Besides the basic fee, there are nominal handling charges, depending upon the agency executing the passport, and added charges for emergency passport service. A person on official business need not pay the passport fee if he has a sponsoring letter.

7. VALIDITY OF PASSPORTS—Passports are valid for five years, unless limited, and may not be renewed. If a passport is lost, the U.S. Department of State should be notified. If it is lost abroad, the owner should report the loss to the U.S. consul.

8. CITIZENSHIP—A naturalized American citizen who visits his homeland may be subject to military service and

other regulations there. The U.S. State Department recommends that such a naturalized citizen get specific information from the consulate of the country of origin before departure.

a. A British citizen who becomes a naturalized American citizen is considered a British citizen by the British government until he makes a formal renunciation of British nationality before the British authorities.

b. A French citizen wishing to become an American citizen is required by French law to have French authorization any time within 15 years of his enrollment in the army unless he has been exempted, has a final discharge, or is over military age, or unless he has fulfilled his military obligations in the U.S. Army during World War I or World War II. An American woman who marries a Frenchman acquires French nationality unless she declines it prior to her marriage.

c. For Israel there are two types of visas: visitor's visas and immigration visas. A visitor's visa is limited to three months and may be renewed. An immigration visa must be obtained by a person who wishes to live in Israel permanently. Such a person must give military service if a male between 18 and 49 inclusive or if a female between 18 and 38 inclusive. Authorization must be obtained from the Ministry of Defense if the person wishes to leave the country before completing military service. Jews who have immigration visas acquire Israeli nationality automatically unless they disavow any intention to the consul of Israel or to the Israeli government.

d. An American citizen who voluntarily joins a foreign army loses his American citizenship unless he has the written consent of the U.S. government to do so.

9. CUSTOMS INFORMATION—Each returning resident of the United States, whether a citizen or not, may bring in merchandise for personal use worth a maximum of $100 free of duty. Members of a family may pool their exemptions if they live in the same household and travel together. The exemption cannot be claimed more often than once in 31 days. Articles purchased abroad and intended to be gifts may be shipped to the United States before or after the return of the U.S. resident. They must be addressed to him or to him in care of some other person and declared in customs. Also, free entry is permitted for bona fide gifts not exceeding $10 in value and sent to persons in the U.S.

Patents

1. DEFINITION—As here used the word *patent* means the granting by the United States to inventors for a limited time the exclusive right to the use, manufacture, and sale of their own inventions. The instrument by which this privilege is confirmed to the inventor is called the *patent* and is issued in the name of the United States of America under the seal of the Patent Office. It is signed by the Secretary of the Interior and countersigned by the Commissioner of Patents.

2. PATENTABLE ITEMS—Any new and useful art, machine, manufacture, or substance may be patented. The patented item may be a completely new invention or discovery, or it may be an "improvement on the art," that is, a new improvement on some existing item. The primary restriction is that the item to be patented must be new; it must not have been sold, used, or known of for any more than a year before patent is applied for. If the discoverer pays all fees and completes the necessary legal proceedings, and if his creation meets the necessary qualifications, he is granted a patent.

3. FOREIGN PATENTS—A person is not debarred from receiving a patent for his invention or discovery by reason of its first having been patented in a foreign country, unless his application for the foreign patent was filed more than twelve months prior to his filing of the application in the United States. In the case of patenting designs, the interval is limited to six months.

4. DURATION OF PATENT—A patent is good for seventeen years, and cannot be extended except by act of Congress. Patents for inventions previously patented in a foreign country must expire at the same time that the foreign patent expires, but in no case shall they be extended more than seventeen years.

5. HOW SECURED—The method of securing patents is by petition, which must be in writing addressed to the Commissioner of Patents. The application must (a) state the name and residence of the petitioner requesting the granting of a patent; (b) designate by title the invention sought to be patented; and (c) contain a reference to the specifications of the invention. It must be signed by the applicant and attested by two witnesses. An alien may obtain a patent on the same terms as a citizen.

6. SPECIFICATIONS—The specifications above referred to are a written description of the invention or discovery, and the manner of making, constructing, composing, and using the same. Specifications are required to be in such full, clear, concise, and exact terms as to enable any person skilled in the art or science to which the invention or discov-

ery appertains to make, construct, compose, and use the same. The inventor or discoverer must point out in particular how his invention or discovery is different from others in the same line. The specifications and claims should be written on but one side of the paper and signed by the applicant. All interlineations and erasures should be avoided.

7. THE OATH—The applicant for a patent must make oath or affirmation that he verily believes himself to be the first and original discoverer of the art, machine, manufacture, composition, other article, or improvement for which he solicits a patent; and that he does not know and does not believe that the same was ever known or used. In addition he should state of what country he is a citizen and where he resides, and whether he is a sole or joint inventor. The oath should be sworn to before a notary public or some other officer authorized to administer oaths.

8. DRAWINGS—The applicant for patent is required also to furnish drawings of his invention whenever the nature of the case admits. Drawings must be signed by the inventor and must be attested by two witnesses; they must show every feature of the invention covered by the claims. When the invention is an improvement on some existing machine, a drawing must exhibit in one or more views the invention itself disconnected from the old structure, and also in another view so much of the old structure as will suffice to show the connection of the invention therewith.

9. MATERIAL—Drawings must be made upon pure white, calendered, smooth, Bristol board of three-sheet thickness. India ink alone must be used. Sheets must be exactly ten by fifteen inches in size. Drawings must be made with pen only, and must be absolutely black. Drawings must be made with the fewest lines possible consistent with clearness. The scale to which a drawing is made must be large enough to show the mechanism without crowding.

10. SIGNATURE of the inventor should be placed at the lower righthand corner of each sheet of drawing and two attesting witnesses should sign at the lower lefthand corner. Drawings should be rolled for transmission to the patent office. The drawings must never be folded.

11. MODEL—A model must be furnished when required by the commissioner.

12. SPECIMENS must be furnished when required by the commissioner.

13. ATTORNEYS—The practice of the Patent Office allows the applicant to retain an attorney, and when the petition is prosecuted by an attorney a power of attorney should be included in the petition. In ordinary cases it is always

best to retain some experienced patent attorney to prosecute the application.

14. CAVEATS—Formerly an inventor could file a *caveat* setting forth the object and distinguishing characteristics of his invention and asking protection for his right until he had finished his invention. This operated for one year. This law was repealed in 1910, so that the only way an inventor can secure any form of federal protection on his patent is by applying for letters patent.

15. FEES—The schedule of fees and prices of publications can be had on application to the Commissioner of Patents, Washington, D.C. For any other information concerning patents an inquiry should be addressed to the Commissioner of Patents.

16. PRELIMINARY EXAMINATIONS—An applicant for a patent may often save considerable expense by having a preliminary examination made of the patents allowed by the Patent Office, to determine whether or not the invention has been patented by somebody else. This examination cannot be made by the Commissioner or anyone of his office, but patent attorneys will make the examination for a small fee.

17. ASSIGNMENTS—Patents may be assigned in whole or in part, and the right to manufacture, sell, and use the patent in any county, state, township, or other district may be granted by the holder of the patent. All such assignments or transfers should be in writing, and are void unless recorded in the Patent Office within three months from their date.

18. FOREIGN PATENT POLICIES—Contrasted with most foreign countries the cost of a patent is very low in the United States, and the law is liberal in allowing the inventor to exploit it. The patent will remain protected even though the invention is not manufactured at all. Some European countries will protect patents only as long as the articles are actually manufactured within their own borders, and as long as the taxes are paid. In the United States foreigners can have their inventions patented without manufacturing them here, and without any taxes whatever.

Payment

1. LEGAL TENDER—In all agreements the payment is to be made in cash unless otherwise stipulated. Since 1933 all coins and currencies of the United States, including Federal Reserve notes, are legal tender for all debts. The United States, however, has ordered that gold coins and certificates payable in gold be exchanged at the Treasury for silver and

silver certificates. Any provision in an obligation that calls for payment in gold is against public policy; the obligation may be discharged by payment in legal tender.

2. CHECKS—In modern times checks are given and received in payment of debts. Legally, however, a check is not payment until it is cashed. In other words, a check is a conditional payment and if the check is not honored, the creditor can sue on the check. He can also sue any of the endorsers whose names appear on the check. But if the holder of the check does not present it for payment within a reasonable time and the bank on which it is drawn fails, he must suffer the loss caused by the delay.

3. NOTES—A note given in payment for a debt may or may not cancel the debt. If the parties intended the note as actual payment, the creditor cannot sue on the original debt; he must sue to recover on the note itself. This is a question of the facts in the case, to be determined by the court.

4. APPLYING PAYMENT WHEN THERE IS MORE THAN ONE DEBT—If a debtor owes more than one debt to the same creditor, he can apply his payments in any way he sees fit. If he fails to do so, the creditor can make the application, and if neither does so, the law applies the payment first to interest due, and then applies the balance to the oldest debt. A signer on a note may insist that payment be applied first to the debt on which he is surety.

5. RECEIPTS—A receipt for a debt is regarded on its face as evidence of payment. This evidence, however, is not conclusive and can sometimes be contradicted by other evidence. For example, suppose A gave B a receipt for $20 and afterwards discovered that the bill B had given him was a counterfeit. A could introduce evidence to prove fraud and thus invalidate the receipt. A contract embodied in a receipt without consideration is not binding, but if there is a valuable consideration, or if the instrument is under seal, such a contract would be as lawful as any other.

Prescriptive Rights or Easements to Title

1. DEFINITION—A *prescriptive right* is a right acquired by use and time and allowed by law.

2. RIGHT OF WAY—A person may acquire a permanent right of way over another's land by passing over that land to his own land for a period of time fixed by law. This right of way cannot be acquired against a minor or against anyone who is incapable of defending his possessions. A person attempting to establish such a right of way can be stopped by appropriate legal action.

3. WAY OF NECESSITY—Sometimes a person sells a part of his farm that is not located on the road. The law allows the purchaser the right to enter and leave the premises, and such a right is called a *way of necessity*. The buyer must exercise reasonable care in selecting his road to the main road, and this road ultimately becomes part of the title to the property.

4. RESTRICTIONS—The law prescribes restrictions on the use of a right of way or a way of necessity. Thus the purchaser of the farm away from the road could not subdivide the farm and transfer his right of way to others without permission of the real owner of the way. However, more than one person can claim a right of way. A tenant can never acquire a right of way beyond the duration of his lease.

5. BUILDING RIGHTS:
a. The owner of a building has no action against one who cuts off his light, air, or view by erecting a building on adjacent land, unless the right has been expressly acquired. The right to light, air, and unobstructed view may sometimes be acquired by deed or by presumption.

   If the owner has acquired such a right, he loses it if he tears down the building and erects a new one.
b. A person has the right to the lateral support of his land. If, for example, a neighbor excavates in an unreasonable manner and a building consequently falls down, the owner has an action against the neighbor and any excavator hired by him.

6. WATER RIGHTS:
a. The water that runs through a person's land may legally be held back for a short time to furnish water power, or it may be used for any other reasonable purpose.
b. Neither a person nor a municipality may dump impurities or sewage into a stream, making the water unfit for use downstream.
c. As a general rule ditches or obstructions may not be dug either to hinder or to hasten the flow of water from one person's land to another in other than the natural way.
d. A riparian owner has the right to cut and sell the ice that forms over the portion of the bed of the stream that he owns, provided he does not interfere with the rights of other owners.
e. A person digging a well cannot be held for cutting off his neighbor's water supply, unless it can be proved that he acted maliciously.

Products Liability

1. DEFINITION — A consumer has a right to products that are reasonably safe. If a product proves to be dangerous, the purchaser may be able to hold the manufacturer or retailer liable for damages. A manufacturer's liability is in general the most extensive created by the law. This liability may be based upon one of four theories: negligence, breach of warranty, strict liability, or misrepresentation.

2. NEGLIGENCE:

a. *Failure to Warn Adequately.* The manufacturer is under a duty to warn of risks with which he is familiar, or with which in the exercise of reasonable care he should have been familiar.

b. *Improper Design.* The manufacturer must so design his product as to make it reasonably safe for its foreseeable uses.

c. *Failure to Test and Inspect Adequately.* The manufacturer is under a duty to turn products out of his production line without unintended defects. There is a breach of this duty where he fails to make reasonable inspections and tests on his product during the course of construction. This includes a duty to make proper tests before the product is first marketed to make sure it will be safe.

3. BREACH OF WARRANTY:

a. *Implied Warranties.* The manufacturer is understood by the marketing of his chattel to make the general implied warranties or promises that his product is both merchantable and reasonably fit for the general uses intended. In the case of food and drugs, this warranty is sometimes called a *warranty of wholesomeness.*

b. *Express Warranty.* If the manufacturer makes an assertion of fact as to the nature, quality, or use of his product, which assertion tends to induce the sale or use of the product, he is exposed by the common law or the sales acts to liability if injury arises proximately from a breach of that warranty or promise.

4. STRICT LIABILITY — *Strict liability* is a new concept, holding the manufacturer liable without fault on his part for injuries arising from the marketing of a product that is defective or unreasonably dangerous.

5. MISREPRESENTATION:

a. *Intentional.* The traditional fraud action in products cases is that against a manufacturer who makes a material misrepresentation of fact that he knows to be false and that he makes with the intent that the injured person rely upon it, if the injured person relies on the misrepresentation to his own injury in ignorance of its falsity. The same liability exists where the statements are made recklessly rather than intentionally.

b.   *Negligent.* Here the manufacturer may be liable, in some states, for making the representation carelessly.

c.   *Innocent.* New section 402B of the Restatement of Torts, 2d, creates liability for injuries arising out of reliance by a person upon representations that are false even though they are made wholly innocently.

6.   RETAILER—The retailer may be liable under any of the four theories listed above, but often his liability is of a narrower scope than that of the manufacturer.

a.   *Negligence.* The retailer is under a duty to warn of the dangers in the use of the products of which he is aware.

b.   *Breach of Warranty.* As a rule the seller makes the same implied warranties as does the manufacturer. This makes him liable for all defects, even though he was under no duty to discover them and even though they might have been latent. A retailer can make an express warranty about his product just as the manufacturer can, and he frequently does make one orally at the point of sale. Where the only express representation comes from the manufacturer, however, as through national advertisement, and all the retailer does is pass on the product without repetition or addition, it is generally recognized that the retailer has no potential liability for breach of express warranty.

c.   *Strict Liability.* Recent cases make it clear that the retailer, like any other supplier, is strictly liable when products are sold in a defective state.

7.   SELLERS OF SECONDHAND GOODS—As a rule, the seller of used goods has the same responsibilities of care as the seller of new goods. For example, where a new car dealer has an obligation to inspect, so does a used car dealer. The liability based upon breach of warranty, however, is much less for the secondhand dealer, partly because the buyer's expectations might be less.

8.   PURCHASERS—The purchaser is the traditional plaintiff. Actions by purchasers today run back against various parties in the distributive chain, and particularly back to the manufacturer of the product involved. There is no requirement that the plaintiff be in a direct contractual relationship with the defendant.

9.   ULTIMATE CONSUMERS—Any consumer can sue for damages, even though he was not the purchaser of the product. The consumer can and does sue anyone in the distributive chain, especially the manufacturer.

10. USERS IN A NONSALE, AMBIGUOUS SALES-SERVICE SITUATION—Often the injured person neither bought the product involved nor got it from someone who had direct dealings with a retailer.

a. *Restaurants.* Almost all courts agree that a restaurant or other place serving food or drink has no defense based on an argument that rather than selling food, it "served" it. If the food is unwholesome, the customer has a breach of warranty action.

b. *Miscellaneous.* Liability has also been held to exist where the product was obtained as a free sample, had been picked out by a prospective purchaser but not yet paid for, or was being tried out by a prospective purchaser.

11. BYSTANDERS—When a defective car goes out of control suddenly, it may injure a pedestrian. The question of the retailer's or manufacturer's liability to the pedestrian is generally analyzed as the liability of the supplier to a "bystander"—someone not in the chain of distribution. Upon reflection it will be seen that any sort of product can injure bystanders, including those products intended for "intimate consumption," such as the hair spray that gets into brother's eye, or the polio vaccine that causes polio in the fetus when the mother takes it for immunization. In negligence actions, there is little hesitation to include the bystander among proper plaintiffs who may sue when injury arises from a defect in a product. The natural limits here would only be those in tort cases generally—zone of the risk and foreseeability of danger.

Professional Men

1. DOCTORS—A *doctor* or *physician* is a person who has (a) been educated in the science of medicine and surgery, (b) been graduated from a medical college, (c) passed the state medical examination, and (d) been licensed by the state to practice his profession.

2. CONFIDENTIAL DISCLOSURES—It frequently happens that a doctor is called upon to give expert testimony in a civil or criminal case. He is not, however, required or permitted to divulge on the witness stand any confidential statement or information obtained in his professional relationship with his patient, except in the following cases:

a. Homicide cases where disclosures relate to homicide.

b. Suits against a doctor for malpractice.

c. Cases in which the patient gives consent for his doctor to testify.

    d.   Suits against insurance companies.

    e.   Will contests.

    f.   Abortion cases.

    g.   Child abuse cases.

    3. LIABILITY — A doctor is not legally liable for the success or failure of his treatment in the absence of an express contract. He is required to exercise the greatest care, diligence, and skill in his work, and can be held criminally liable only for carelessness and gross negligence. The crime of malpractice consists of any injurious or improper treatment.

    4. LAWYERS — A *lawyer* is a person who has (a) been educated in the science of law, (b) been graduated from a law school or, in a few states, been apprenticed to an attorney, and (c) passed the state bar examination. Every man is entitled by law to have a lawyer represent him in his trial, but the court will furnish the services of a lawyer only in criminal cases and certain civil cases.

    5. CONFIDENTIAL DISCLOSURES — What has already been said about the confidential relationship existing between doctors and patients applies even more strongly to attorneys and their clients. The matters spoken of between them are confidential; no law can force the lawyer to divulge them on the witness stand.

    6. LIENS — An attorney has a lien for the payment of his fee on all documents, moneys, and other things coming into his possession.

    7. LIABILITY — A lawyer cannot be held liable for the failure of his case unless he did not exercise reasonable care and judgment.

Real Property Transactions

    1. DEFINITION — *Real property* is land and anything permanently attached to it. This includes not only buildings and their fixtures, but also plants, minerals beneath the land, and the air space above it.

    2. CONTRACTS OF SALE — An agreement to purchase real estate must be in writing and should be signed by both buyer and seller. The writing need not mention the amount to be paid for the land. It should be signed in ink, but is not invalid if signed with a lead pencil or even with a rubber stamp. The entire contract need not be on the same sheet of paper, and it sometimes happens that two or more sheets of paper constitute the contract, as in cases where the agreement to purchase land is completed through correspondence between the two parties. See also CONTRACTS.

3. ORAL AGREEMENTS are not binding in the sale of real property. For example, if a purchaser makes an oral agreement to purchase land and pays part of the purchase price, he cannot compel the seller to give him a deed to the real estate. The purchaser can, however, compel the seller to return the money he has paid down.

4. EXCEPTIONS—There are some exceptions to the rule that oral agreements in real estate transactions are unenforceable. For example, A sells a piece of property to B, receives the purchase price, and without written agreement allows B to take possession of the property. If B makes valuable and lasting improvements on the property, the courts will compel A to give B a deed to the property. Generally, if the acts of the buyer and seller provide strong evidence that a contract exists, or if the buyer has made substantial improvements in the property, the courts will enforce an oral contract.

5. OPTIONS—An *option* is a contract by which the owner of property agrees that the other party shall have the right to purchase the property at a fixed price within a certain time. For example, A agrees to sell a piece of property to B for $10,000 within six months, for which B gives A a valuable consideration. B must either exercise his option and purchase the property before six months pass or forfeit his consideration. All options must be in writing. If no time limit is fixed in the agreement, the option must be exercised within a reasonable time.

6. TRANSFER OF TITLE—In most real estate contracts the seller agrees to furnish the buyer with a good and merchantable title. He also agrees to transfer title to the property by a warranty deed, which warrants the title in him and the buyer against any loss that might be occasioned by defects in the title. A purchaser should always insist that the contract provide that the seller is to furnish and deliver a merchantable title. The contract should also require the seller to furnish evidence that he has good title. This is done by producing either an abstract, guaranty policy, or Torrens certificate showing good title in the seller. See also DEEDS: WARRANTY DEEDS.

7. ABSTRACT OF TITLE—An *abstract* is a statement in substance of what appears in the public records affecting the title to the land in question from the time it was owned by the government down to date. The public records are searched and the matters shown therein. An abstract will show all transfers, mortgages, judgments, tax sales, liens of all kinds, court proceedings, and everything of record affecting the title to the property. These abstracts are prepared by

private concerns or individuals known as *abstract compa-nies* or *abstracters*. To determine whether or not the seller's title is good, the purchaser should have the abstract examined by an attorney competent to pass upon the law of real property. This examination by an attorney will reveal the validity or merchantability of the title. The objections to a clear title may be simple or exceedingly complex, and require the services of a competent attorney in that field. Usually the seller pays all of the expenses incidental to bringing the abstract up to date. The purchaser generally pays the examination fee.

8. TITLE INSURANCE OR GUARANTY POLICY — Under this system the title company issues a policy guaranteeing the holder of the policy against any loss he might sustain by reason of any defect in the title, whether of record or otherwise, existing before or at the time of the issuance of the policy. This system is becoming more popular in cities because of the demand for facilities to expedite real estate transactions and also because of the system's protective features.

9. TORRENS SYSTEM — The *Torrens system* is a system providing for the registration of land titles in such a manner that, when the title is once registered, a certificate of the registrar of titles will show the exact condition of the title. In order to register a title under this system, it is necessary that a court proceeding be had first in which the decree of the court settles and establishes the title. After this has been done, the registrar of titles will issue an official certificate that will show who has title to the land, and what defects, if any, appear in his title. After the title to a particular parcel of property has been so registered, all subsequent transactions affecting the title to that property must be filed with the registrar of titles, and are noted upon the certificate of title. This enables a purchaser to determine the true state of the title by merely examining the certificate of the registrar. The purpose of the system is to simplify the transfer of real estate, and it is now in force in a number of states.

10. FORMS:

CONTRACT FOR SALE OF LAND

This agreement, made and entered into this . . . . . . day of . . . . . by and between . . . ., party of the first part, and . . . ., party of the second part, witnesseth:

1. The said party of the first part, for and in con-

sideration of the sum of $ .... to be paid as hereinafter provided, hereby agrees to sell unto the party of the second part the following described tract of land:

|Description|

2. The said party of the second part hereby agrees to purchase said premises at said consideration of $......., and to pay the same as follows: (set out terms of payment).

3. The said party of the first part, upon receiving the final payment mentioned above, shall execute and deliver to the said party of the second part, or to his assigns, a duly acknowledged Warranty Deed, conveying to him or them the fee simple title to said premises, free and clear from all incumbrance.

In witness whereof the said parties have hereunto set their hands and seals the day and year first above written.

OPTION

For and in consideration of the sum of .... dollars to me in hand paid, the receipt whereof is hereby acknowledged, I hereby grant unto .... an option for ...... days from the .... day of ...., 19 ....., to purchase for the sum of .... dollars, the following described lands situated in the County of .... and State of ....

|Insert description of property|

upon the following terms and conditions: (insert terms of sale), said .... to signify his intention to take or reject the same by due notice in writing within the time above specified, and a failure to serve such notice within the time specified shall terminate this option without further action, time being the essence of this agreement.

In case said notice shall be served in due time, then thirty days shall be given in which to examine abstract or other evidence of title, and close the sale.

Sale and Transfer of Property

1. DEFINITIONS—A *sale* is the exchange of property for a consideration called the *price,* which is either to be paid at once or at some future date. An agreement to sell at a future date is called an *executory sale.* A present sale is called an

executed sale. A sale may be made either in writing or orally. The following general principles apply to sales.

a. Sales are based on mutual agreement.

b. Either the thing sold must exist at the time of the sale or there must be reason to believe that it will be in existence and in possession of the seller. For example: if a man sold a horse for $100 and the horse died before the actual time of the sale, the transaction would not be a sale.

c. Grain or other produce not yet sowed or planted can be sold because the seller may reasonably expect a crop. Machinery or other manufactured goods may be sold before they are made and the seller can be held to perform his part of the contract as though the articles actually existed at the time of the sale.

d. The thing sold must be specified and set apart as the property of the buyer in order to complete the sale.

e. When nothing is said as to the time of payment when the sale is made, the law presumes that the property must be paid for before the purchaser can secure possession. If credit is agreed upon, the buyer is entitled to immediate possession.

f. When goods are sold on *sale or return* the title passes to the buyer when he signifies his approval or when he keeps them beyond the time set for their return.

g. When no price is fixed in the agreement, the purchaser must pay a reasonable price.

h. Goods are often sold and shipped subject to bill of lading; that is, payment is not made until the goods are delivered. Thus the seller controls the property until it is paid for, although the title may pass to the buyer.

2. STATUTE OF FRAUDS—The Uniform Commercial Code provides that a contract to sell $500 worth of goods or more cannot be enforced unless the purchaser advances a sum of money to bind the bargain, or unless the contract is in writing. This rule, of course, does not apply when the goods sold are to be manufactured especially for the buyer and would not be readily salable to others.

3. RELIEVING THE BUYER—The buyer's obligation is limited in various ways. For instance, the contract may be voided (a) if the goods purchased have been damaged or destroyed before delivery, or (b) if in the buyer's opinion the goods are not satisfactory.

4. WARRANTIES—When goods are sold there are certain warranties by the seller that may be either expressed or implied. Any statement made by the seller tending to induce the buyer to purchase is an express warranty. In every sale

there are implied warranties that the seller has the title to the property, and that the goods will correspond with the description or sample. Any defects that can be seen in property when sold do not relieve the buyer from meeting his contract though he claims that he did not see the defects. The law does not furnish eyes for the purchaser of property. But defects in property that cannot be seen and of which the seller makes no statement release the buyer from his contract. See also TRUTH IN ADVERTISING; PRODUCTS LIABILITY.

5.   THE BULK SALES LAW is a part of the law of many states. It provides that when a stock of goods or merchandise is sold, transferred, or consigned in bulk, the seller's creditors must be notified in writing a certain number of days before the sale is completed. Thus when a merchant sells his merchandise in bulk, the buyer should keep the following considerations in mind: First, he should demand a bill of sale. Second, he should either demand an affidavit from the seller that he has notified the creditors, or secure a sworn list of the creditors and notify them himself. This law applies to corporations, partnerships, and individuals, and any attempt to evade its provisions carries with it a penalty of a fine, a year's imprisonment, or both. If the creditors are not properly notified they can hold the purchaser liable for the debts.

6.   STOCK MARKET SPECULATION — Trading in stocks, grains, and cotton, together with the buying and selling of futures, is now largely regulated by statute. A contract of this kind which involves the actual delivery of property is perfectly legal, even if the seller did not own the property at the time the sale was made. However, when no exchange of property is ever contemplated and the parties merely propose to effect a settlement based on the market changes, the contract is not legal.

7.   FORMS:

BILL OF SALE

Know all men by these presents, That I, ... of . . . ., County . . . ., in consideration of Six Hundred Dollars ($600) to me in hand paid by . . . . of the same place, the receipt of which is hereby acknowledged, do hereby grant, sell, assign, transfer, and deliver unto the said . . . ., his heirs and assigns, the following goods and chattels, to wit:

Four Yearling Heifers, at $50 each	$200
30 head of Sheep, at $4 each	120
Five sets of Harness, at $20 each	100

Two Farm Wagons, at $35 each 70
One Corn Planter, at $20 20
Six Plows, at $15 each.................... 90

To have and to hold all of the said goods and chattels to the said ...., his heirs and assigns forever. And I do hereby covenant to and with the said .... that I am the legal owner of said goods and chattels; that they are free and clear from all other and prior sales and incumbrances; that I have good right to sell and convey the same as aforesaid, and that in the peaceable possession of the said .... I will forever warrant and defend the same against the lawful claims and demands of all persons whomsoever.

In witness whereof, I have hereunto set my hand and seal this 29th day of June, A.D. 19 ....

In the presence of

....

....

(Signed) .... (Seal)

Note: In selling or buying automobiles, especially used cars, it is always wise to insert the name of the machine, its model, the engine number, the car number, the type of car, its color, and any other information that will help to identify it.

Secured Transactions

1. DEFINITION — A *secured credit sale* is a sale in which the possession of the goods and the risk of loss pass to the buyer, but the seller retains a security interest in the goods until he has been paid in full. The seller's security interest entitles him to repossess the goods when the buyer fails to make payments as required or when in any other way the buyer commits a breach of the purchase contract. This right of repossession is in addition to the right to sue on the purchase contract for the amount of the purchase price. A security interest for the protection of the seller arises as soon as the seller and buyer agree that the buyer shall have property rights in particular goods and that the seller shall have a security interest in them. It is immaterial whether or not the sales agreement provides for the passage of title to the buyer prior to his payment in full for the goods.

2. SECURITY AGREEMENT — The agreement of the seller and buyer that the seller shall have a security interest in the goods must be evidenced by a written *security agreement*,

which is signed by the buyer and which describes the collateral. This description need only reasonably identify the collateral. A description is sufficient when it would enable a third person, aided by inquires made to others, to determine what goods were involved.

3. RIGHTS OF SELLER INDEPENDENT OF DEFAULT—The seller may transfer or assign his interest under the sales contract and under the security agreement to a third person, and the assignee acquires all the rights and interest of the seller. As soon as the security agreement is executed, the secured credit seller of consumer goods has rights that are effective not only against the buyer but also against purchasers of the property from the buyer. From that moment on, the seller's interest is generally effective against third persons and is described as a *perfected security interest.*

4. FILING—In an ordinary sale of consumer goods under a secured transaction, no filing is required in order to perfect the secured seller's interest. Such a seller is protected against purchasers from and creditors of the buyer who may acquire the property thereafter. Although this is the general rule, there are some exceptions:

a. The seller's security interest is not perfected, and filing is required to perfect it, if the goods purchased are to be attached to buildings or land as a fixture or if they consist of farm equipment sold for a purchase price of over $2,500.

b. A security interest in a motor vehicle required to be licensed is not perfected unless the vehicle is licensed with a notation of the security interest made in the title certificate, if such is required by law. If the law does not require this notation on the title, the seller must file his security interest in order to perfect it.

5. RIGHTS OF THE BUYER—The buyer has certain rights of ownership in the collateral. It is not material whether technically he is the owner of the title. Whatever interest he owns he may transfer voluntarily, and his creditors may reach it by the process of the law as fully as though there were no security agreement. Such third persons generally cannot acquire any greater rights than the buyer, and therefore they hold the property subject to the security interest of the seller.

It is common practice for credit sellers to seek to protect themselves by prohibiting the buyer from reselling the property. Such a provision has no effect and does not prevent an effective resale, even though the security agreement expressly makes it a default or breach of the contract to make a resale.

6. BUYER'S RIGHTS AS A DEBTOR —The secured transaction buyer is a debtor to the extent that there is a balance due on the purchase price. In order for the buyer to know just how much he owes and to check with his own records what the seller claims to to be due, the buyer has the right to compel the seller to state what balance is owed and also to specify in what collateral the seller claims a security interest.

7. WAIVER OF DEFENSES—It is common practice for finance companies that have a standing agreement to purchase sales contracts from a credit seller to provide him with forms to be signed by the buyer. These forms generally specify that the buyer waives, as against the assignee of the sales contract and security agreement, any right that he would have against the seller. Both express and implied waivers are valid and bind the buyer if the assignee takes his assignment for value, in good faith, and without notice or knowledge of any claim or defense of the buyer. The validity of any waiver of defense is subject to two limitations:

a.   Those defenses that could be raised against the holder in due course of commercial paper cannot be waived.

b.   The waiver is not effective if a statute or decision establishes a different rule for buyers of consumer goods.

8. REPOSSESSION—When the buyer under the secured credit sale defaults by failing to pay an installment due, the secured party is entitled to take the collateral or purchased property from the buyer. If he can do so without causing a breach of the peace, the seller may repossess the property without legal proceedings. In any case he may use legal proceedings if he desires.

9. RESALE OF COLLATERAL—The seller who has repossessed the goods may resell them at a private or public sale at any time and place and on any terms. He must, however, act in good faith and in a manner that is commercially reasonable. The seller must give the buyer reasonable advance notice of a resale unless the goods are perishable, or unless they threaten to decline speedily in value, or unless they are of a type customarily sold on a recognized market. The seller's resale destroys all interest of the buyer in the goods.

10. REDEMPTION OF COLLATERAL—If the buyer acts in time, he may redeem or obtain the return to him of the goods by tendering to the secured party the amount that is owed him, including expenses and any legal costs that have been incurred. The right to redeem is destroyed if the seller has made a resale or entered into a binding contract for resale.

11.   ACCOUNTING AFTER RESALE—When the secured party, that is, the original seller, makes a resale of repossessed goods, the proceeds of the resale are applied in the following order to pay (a) reasonable costs of repossession, storage, and resale of the goods, (b) the balance due, including interest and any proper additions such as attorney's fees, and (c) subsequent security interests on the property that are discharged by the resale. If any balance remains after the payment of these claims, the buyer is entitled to the surplus. Conversely, if the net proceeds of resale are insufficient to pay the costs and the debt due the seller, the buyer is liable for such deficiency unless it has been otherwise agreed by the parties.

12.   RETENTION OF COLLATERAL—If the buyer has paid less than 60 percent of the cash price of the consumer goods, the secured seller may propose in writing that he, the seller, keep the repossessed collateral in payment of the debt. If the buyer does not object to this proposal, the secured party keeps the collateral and the secured obligation is automatically discharged. If the buyer makes written objection to the proposal within 30 days, the secured party must then proceed to dispose of the collateral by resale or other reasonable manner.

13.   SECURED CREDIT SALES OF INVENTORY—In contrast with one who buys personal property for his own use, the buyer may be a merchant or dealer who intends to resell the goods. The goods that such a merchant or dealer buys are classified as *inventory*. Filing of a *financing statement* is required to perfect the creditor's interest in inventory or the proceeds therefrom. An exception is made when a statute, such as a motor vehicle statute, requires the security interest to be noted on the title certificate issued for the property.

14.   FINANCING STATEMENT— The financing statement is distinct from the security agreement that was executed by the parties to give rise to the secured transaction. The financing statement must be signed by both the debtor and the secured party; it must give an address of the secured party, from which information concerning the security interest may be obtained, and a mailing address of the debtor; and it must contain a statement indicating the types, or describing the items, of collateral.

15.   PROTECTION OF CUSTOMER OF THE BUYER—The customer of the buyer takes the goods free from the secured interest of the secured party. That is, one who buys in the ordinary course of business items of property taken from the original buyer's inventory is free from the secured party's interest, even though that interest was perfected and even

though such ultimate customer knew of the secured party's interest.

16. RIGHTS AND REMEDIES AFTER DEFAULT—The rights and remedies of the secured party and the buyer of inventory after a default on the part of the latter are similar to those in the case of a secured credit sale of consumer goods.

Securities Law

1. DEFINITION—Stocks, bonds, and notes are commonly called *securities*, but this term has received an expanded interpretation by the courts. It clearly covers not only stocks, bonds, and notes, but any offering that constitutes an investment, regardless of form. It covers monies paid over as loans, such as bonds, debentures, or promissory notes, as well as purchases of equity or ownership interests.

2. STATE REGULATION OF SECURITIES —Nearly every state has some kind of "blue sky" law, that is, a law designed to regulate and supervise the issuance and selling of securities. Such laws were first written to outlaw the sale of stock in fraudulent corporations whose primary asset was the "blue sky." The laws' main function now is to assure disclosure of all material facts about securities that are offered for sale. Several types of these laws are in effect:

a. *Fraud.* The simplest are laws that simply impose civil or criminal sanctions for any fraud in connection with the sale or issuance of securities.

b. *Registration.* Other laws require that the stock be registered with an appropriate state officer or agency prior to issuance. The registration must contain a complete description of the issuance, and the shares must be sold as so described. The purpose of this type of statute is simply disclosure. There is generally no discretion in the state to deny permission to issue.

c. *Permit.* The most advanced and complex type of blue sky law is the permit or license type, which in effect provides that no stock may be issued until a permit is obtained.

3. FEDERAL REGULATION OF SECURITIES—The Securities Act of 1933 and the Securities Exchange Act of 1934 provide the basic framework for federal regulation of the sale of securities in interstate commerce. The 1933 act deals with initial issuance of shares, while the 1934 act is aimed principally at sales by underwriters, on stock exchanges, etc. These acts provide for a *registration* system of regulation, the purpose of which is to assure a full disclosure of all pertinent facts to any prospective investor.

4.   SECURITIES ACT OF 1933—The 1933 act prohibits the offer or sale of nonexempt securities to the public in interstate commerce unless and until a registration statement has been filed with the Securities and Exchange Commission. The S.E.C. has no power to disapprove or veto a proposed issuance. Its only power is to compel disclosure of all pertinent details. The following types of transactions are expressly exempted from the 1933 act:

a.   *Sale by Private Investor.* Any transaction by a person who is the owner of the shares is exempt. Such is deemed a casual sale, not a public offering.

b.   *Private Offering.* Sales or issuance by the corporation to a specific, limited number of private subscribers, usually no more than 25, are exempt as long as no resale to the public is contemplated.

c.   *Intrastate Transactions.* Where the sale or issuance is entirely intrastate, that is, when the seller and the purchaser are both bona fide residents of the same state and no interstate mail or communications are used to advertise or effect the sale of issue, federal law does not apply.

d.   *Small Issues.* Where the total amount of the issue is under $300,000 an abbreviated registration statement is accepted in lieu of the more detailed statement otherwise required.

5.   REGISTRATION STATEMENT—The corporation must file with the S.E.C. a statement of all matters pertaining to the proposed issuance. The form required is designed to force disclosure of all factors that may affect the fairness of the issue and the financial status of the corporation. Full details must be provided as to the identity and background of all corporate officers and directors, the compensation they receive, the sales costs, underwriting commission and discounts, and other relevant matters.

6.   FRAUD IN THE REGISTRATION STATEMENT—Where the registration statement filed contains a misstatement or omission of material fact, the holder of the securities is entitled to maintain an action for damages, that is, the amount he lost on the investment, against all persons connected with the issuance. In effect, absolute liability is imposed. The holder does not have to prove fraud in the torts sense or show that he relied on the misstatement. The holder need not even prove that the misstatement caused the decline in the value of the securities. The liability for damages extends not only to the corporation, and any underwriter, but to all persons who signed the registration statement, or who were directors or partners of the issuer at

the time the registration statement was filed, or who were named therein as prospective directors or partners. If any accountant or other expert certifies portions of the registration statement which are false or misleading, he is liable.

7. FRAUD OTHER THAN IN REGISTRATION STATEMENT —The 1933 act also provides a right of action in favor of the original buyer of a security for an untrue statement or omission of material fact in any transaction connected with the issuance of the security, where the misstatement or omission is either intentional or could have been avoided by exercise of due diligence. Liability here extends to misrepresentations in the offering prospectus or any oral misstatements by the issuer, as well as to any misstatement in the registration statement filed with the S.E.C.

8. SECURITIES EXCHANGE ACT OF 1934—The 1934 act requires registration of any stock that is traded on a national securities exchange, or in any over-the-counter market, if the corporation has total assets exceeding $1,000,000 and a class of equity security held by 500 or more persons. A corporation so qualified must file continuing periodic reports with the S.E.C. as to all of the various matters that may affect the financial status of the corporation and its outstanding securities. The most important provision of the 1934 act in regard to the issuance of securities is Section 10b which provides that it is unlawful "to use or employ . . . any manipulative or deceptive device" in connection with the purchase or sale of any security.

9. RULE 10b-5—To execute Sec. 10b, the S.E.C. promulgated Rule 10b-5, which, in effect, makes it unlawful for any person, in connection with the purchase or sale of any security, (a) to employ any device to defraud, (b) to make any untrue statement of a material fact, (c) to omit to state a material fact necessary in order to make the statements made not misleading, or (d) to engage in any act, practice or course of business that would operate as fraud or deceit upon any person. Rule 10b-5 applies to any person; it is not limited to officers, directors, and controlling shareholders of the issuer who are ordinarily considered to be "insiders." Securities of all issuers are covered by the rule; thus, the prescriptions of Rule 10b-5 apply to the securities of small, closely held corporations as well as to the securities of publicly owned corporations.

10. REMEDY—In addition to action taken by the S.E.C. pursuant to Rule 10b-5, whether for injunction against an issuer or relief of allegedly defrauded persons, a private party may also bring a civil suit in the federal courts based upon an alleged violation of the rule. Although neither the

1934 act nor the rule itself specifically affords a civil remedy, the courts have consistently found one. Many courts
have construed Rule 10b-5 liberally in favor of investors
and, although it is a fraud rule, they have either watered
down or discarded some of the elements necessary to prove
common-law fraud.

11. SHORT-TERM PROFITS BY INSIDERS—Section 16b of the
Securities Exchange Act of 1934 creates a conclusive
presumption that any gain from short-term transactions is
the result of "inside information." The section provides that
any profits made by a director or a ten-percent shareholder
as the result of any purchase and sale of a registered security that take place within six months of each other belong to
the corporation. The purpose is to discourage persons who
have access to special information from taking advantage of
their position.

Shipping

1. REGISTRATION—The law requires all ships flying the
United States flag to file papers with the collector of
customs in the district where the ship's home port is situated. This formality is called *registration* for ships engaged
in foreign trade, *enrollment* in the case of large ships engaged in coastwise or internal commerce, and *license* for
smaller ships.

2. OWNERSHIP—Vessels may be owned by individuals,
partnerships, or corporations, and the ownership may be acquired either by purchase or construction. If several individuals own a ship, they are tenants in common where
there is no other relation between the part owners of a
vessel than that arising out of joint ownership. Each part
owner has his share of the profits and expenses, and no one
individual can bind the others except for the necessary
maintenance of the ship. When a partnership or corporation
owns a vessel, the ordinary rules of corporations and partnerships apply.

3. SALE—The owner of a ship can sell or mortgage his interest at any time, but in order to effect a good title against
third parties the contract should be in writing. If a ship is
sold while it is at sea, the buyer takes it subject to all contracts made by the master before learning of the sale. In all
other cases the buyer is not liable for repairs made or supplies furnished previous to the sale.

4. MARITIME LOANS—In cases of great emergency, for
example when a ship is in a foreign port without funds to
purchase necessary supplies, a master can secure a
maritime loan in which the vessel is put up as security. If

the vessel fails to reach home the lender loses his money, but in the event of a safe arrival he has the boat as security and can hold the master personally. Such a contract calls for a high rate of interest but is perfectly legal. The technical name for the contract is *contract of bottomry*.

5. THE MASTER of a vessel is the chief officer. The law gives him authority to bind the owners for necessary repairs or supplies. He must render accurate accounts of his actions and money received, but his first duty is to the passengers and the crew. He has the power to regulate their actions in any manner that is necessary to their safety, comfort, and good order. If on account of illness, insanity, or other reason, the master is unable to perform his duties properly, those duties pass to the lower officers in the order of their rank.

6. THE SEAMEN—Statutes and maritime law generally require the execution of shipping papers between the master and the seamen before starting on a voyage to a foreign country or from one state to another. These articles must specify:

a. The exact nature of the voyage.
b. The destination.
c. The duration.
d. The amount of wages to be paid each seaman.

If shipping articles are not properly executed, or if the master violates the contract, the seaman can leave the ship and recover the highest rate of wages, his expenses home, and damages. On the other hand, a seaman may be discharged for reasons that show him to be unfit for the service or to be trusted in the vessel, such as long-continued disobedience, drunkenness, or incapacity due to his own conduct.

7. COURTS OF ADMIRALTY have jurisdiction over all maritime contracts, torts, injuries, or offenses.

Statutes of Limitation

1. DEFINITION—A *statute of limitation* is a law that specifies the time after which debts or actions are no longer enforceable. All states have such laws providing different periods of time, varying from one to twenty years, within which legal actions must be brought before the courts are closed to them.

2. COMPUTING TIME—Time is computed from the date the debt is incurred or, in accounts, from the date of the last purchase or from the time of the injury complained of. The debt may be renewed by a partial payment of principal or interest, or by a written acknowledgment in a note or paper, with an expressed willingness to pay indicated by the debtor.

Torts or Wrongs

1. DEFINITION—A *tort* is a private or civil wrong or injury arising independent of contract. The proper remedy is an action for damages.

2. TORTS AND CRIMES—There is a distinction between torts and crimes. If a wrongful act violates a private right it is a *tort;* if it violates a public right it is a *crime.* Very frequently the wrongful act is in violation of both private and public rights. In such cases, even if the wrongdoer makes personal restitution or settlement with the person wronged, the state still has the right to punish the wrongdoer for the crime. Suppose A steals $500 from B, who finds it out and succeeds in getting A to return the money. A has still committed a crime against the public and can be punished as the law provides.

3. ASSAULT AND BATTERY—A person who intentionally invades the person of another by physical contact, or puts him in apprehension of an invasion of his person by threat of immediate physical contact, without such person's consent, and not in reasonable defense of person or other interest, and not in the performance of some duty imposed by law, or the exercise of some privilege by reason of the relation of the parties, is liable in damages. A successful assault becomes a battery when the injury is actually done.

a. Every person is entitled by law to liberty, security of life, and security of his property.

b. Mere words do not constitute an assault.

c. The wrong consists not so much in the actual striking of the person as in the manner and spirit of the act.

d. Accidental injury is not a battery.

e. A blow unlawfully aimed at one person but striking another is a battery.

f. Reasonable methods of self-defense may be employed in resisting a battery and in defending either a member of one's family or one's property.

4. DEFAMATION—A *defamation* is a false and malicious imputation of bad character or reputation either by slander or by libel.

a. Every person has a right to his good reputation.

b. Every person is assumed to have a good reputation until the contrary is proved.

c. *Slander* is oral defamation.

d. *Libel* is defamation in writing or printing.

5. SLANDER—In simple words, this tort consists of speaking words in another's hearing that injure a third person's reputation. The United States Supreme Court has classified

slanderous words that are objectionable:

a. Words falsely spoken of a person that impute to the party the commission of some criminal offense involving moral turpitude for which the party, if the charge is true, may be indicted and punished.

b. Words falsely spoken of a person that impute that the party is infected with some infectious disease, which, if the charge is true, would exclude the party from society.

c. Defamatory words spoken of a party that impute to the party unfitness to perform the duties of an office or employment for profit, or the want of integrity in the discharge of the duties of such an office or employment.

d. Defamatory words falsely spoken of a party that prejudice such party in his or her profession or trade.

e. Defamatory words falsely spoken of a person that, though not in themselves actionable, occasion the party special damage.

6. LIBEL.—It is even more dangerous to defame a person's character in writing. Many words when written or printed are libelous, which if spoken would not be slanderous without proof of special injury.

a. The owners of books and newspapers generally are liable for the publication of libelous matter, even though printed without their knowledge and even against their orders.

b. News dealers are immune from any liability for selling or displaying newspapers or magazines that contain libelous matter, providing such dealers have no knowledge of the libelous matter.

c. In order to hold the editor or proprietor of the printing plant, the injured party must prove that the libelous matter could be recognized by an intelligent person as libel.

7. DEFENSES AGAINST CHARGES OF DEFAMATION are given below:

a. The truth of the charge is generally a complete defense against an action for damages. Statutes, however, sometimes require that not only must the words be true, but they must also be uttered in good faith.

b. A privileged communication, such as what is said or written in a judicial proceeding or in a legitimate newspaper report thereof, is not held to be libelous matter. This privilege extends to the heads of the executive departments of government. Statements rendered by mercantile agencies and the reports of many semi-public societies are also conditionally privileged.

c.   Fair comment is still another defense. The conduct of public men is held to be a proper matter for public discussion, so long as the writer keeps within the bounds of an honest intention to discharge a duty to the public, and does not make the occasion a mere cover for false allegations. The same rule applies to newspaper reports of literary or artistic productions offered to the public.

8.   FALSE IMPRISONMENT is a crime, and the person unlawfully imprisoned has the right to a civil action for damages. The defense may be that the officer was clothed with the proper authority and acted upon probable cause. In a case involving parent and child, guardian and ward, or teacher and pupil, it may be shown that the alleged wrongdoer was acting within his duty.

9.   MALICIOUS PROSECUTION is another wrong. This is the malicious instituting of suit without probable cause, and both the malice and the lack of probable cause must be proved. A suit to recover for this wrong cannot be started before the alleged malicious prosecution has come to an end. That the accused party acted on the advice of his attorney after a full and fair disclosure of the facts is a good defense against a charge of malicious prosecution.

10.   CONSPIRACY—A conspiracy is a combination of two or more persons to accomplish an unlawful end that is injurious to another. Thus members of a trade union may lawfully agree that they will stop work, or that they will not work with certain other laborers, but they commit a wrong as soon as they interfere with the liberty of others. Employers who combine to use unlawful methods to exclude a certain class of workmen are also guilty of a wrong. An agreement among manufacturers that they will all operate as the majority agree may be a conspiracy in restraint of trade.

11.   SEARCH AND SEIZURE—It is unlawful to search private premises unless a search warrant has been issued by proper authority. It is a criminal offense to open another's letters, or to retain or pry into them. The federal and state constitutions protect persons against unreasonable searches and seizures.

12.   NUISANCES—A *nuisance* is anything wrongfully done or permitted that injures or annoys another in the enjoyment of his legal rights. Below is a list of some of the nuisances subject to an action in tort:

a.   To remove or weaken the lateral support of the adjoining land.

b.   To mine or tunnel under another's land without providing suitable support.

c. To extend buildings over another's land.
d. To allow filthy deposits to accumulate on one's property.
e. To deposit refuse in a stream of water.
f. To erect a dam, backing up the water to injure the land of another.
g. To use or care for explosives, loaded weapons, or dangerous machines in a negligent manner.
h. To conduct a place of business or amusement, or engage in any activity, in a way that will materially interfere with the ordinary physical comfort of others.
i. To allow poisonous or offensive materials to remain in a place where they may cause injury to others.
j. To put or allow a heavy article or substance to remain where it is likely to fall and injure persons or property.
k. To erect, operate, and maintain electrical appliances without reasonable care in proportion to their danger.
l. For a state, county, or municipality to allow defects in streets, highways, or sidewalks that result in injury to persons or property.

Trademarks

1. DEFINITION—A *trademark* is an emblem or symbol to designate the goods of a merchant or manufacturer. The owner of a trademark may have it registered in the U.S. Patent Office and thus acquire the right to keep others from using it.

2. REGISTRATION—The first step of trademark registration is to file or sign an application addressed to the Commissioner of Patents. This application must include

a. The name, domicile, location, and citizenship of applicant.
b. A description of the goods for which trademark is used.
c. The method of affixing trademark.
d. Length of time the trademark has been used.
e. Description of trademark.
f. Drawing and specimens of the trademark.

The next step is the payment of a fee for registration.

3. REGISTER—There are two registers of the U.S. Patent Office on which trademarks may be registered. To be registered on the Principal Register, the trademark must be coined, arbitrary, fanciful, or suggestive; these are usually called *technical marks*. If the trademark is merely descriptive of goods or their regional origin or is primarily a surname, it is placed on the Supplemental Register.

4. LENGTH OF TIME A TRADEMARK IS PROTECTED—The registration of a trademark remains in force for twenty

years. It may be renewed for a period of twenty years if it is still used in trade regulated by the U.S. Congress. The fee for renewal is $25. A trademark may be canceled or surrendered. It is canceled if within one year next preceding the expiration of six years from the date of registration the applicant fails to file an affidavit either affirming that he is using the mark or showing that he has reason for nonuse. Unless the affidavit is filed, the registration is canceled after six years.

5. RESTRICTIONS—The law has placed certain restrictions on the registration of trademarks. For example, it is impossible to register a trademark if

a. It comprises immoral, deceptive, or scandalous matter.
b. It contains matter that may disparage or falsely suggest a connection with persons living or dead.
c. It contains matter that may disparage or falsely suggest a connection with institutions, beliefs, or national symbols.
d. It consists of, or includes, the flag or coat of arms or other insignia of the United States, any state, municipality, or foreign nation.
e. It uses, without his consent, the portrait, signature, or name of a living person, or those of a deceased President of the United States without consent of his widow.

6. REGISTRATION OF OTHER MARKS —The law provides for the registration of service marks, certification marks, and collective marks. A *service mark* is a mark used in the sale or advertising of services to identify the services of one person and distinguish them from the services of others. A *certification mark* is used to certify origin or quality of goods; an example is a union label. A *collective mark* is used by an association, such as a cooperative.

7. ADDITIONAL INFORMATION—A pamphlet, *General Information Concerning Trademarks,* is available from the U.S. Patent Office, Washington, D.C. 20025. It describes the way applications and drawings are to be prepared and gives sample forms for applications. The Official Gazette contains information on trademarks registered, renewed, or published for opposition.

Truth in Advertising

1. DEFINITION—*Advertising* is any public statement, whether written, filmed, or spoken, that is designed to attract public attention. Any assertion made in an advertisement becomes a warranty; it must not mislead the public. In

FTC v. *Algoma Lumber Co.*, the United States Supreme Court derived from the Federal Trade Commission Act a rule that "the public is entitled to get what it chooses, though the choice may be dictated by caprice or by fashion or perhaps by ignorance." In advertising, nothing less than the most literal truthfulness is tolerated.

2. APPLICATION OF PRINCIPLE—This principle has been interpreted as forbidding a businessman (a) to state falsely that his product ordinarily sells for a higher price but is offered at a bargain, even if the purchaser is in fact receiving his money's worth; (b) to misrepresent to the public that he is in a certain line of business, even though the misstatement bears no relationship to the quality of his product; (c) to merchandise reprocessed products without disclosing that they are "used," even if they are functionally identical with new products; (d) to misappropriate another's trademark; (e) to state falsely that a product has received a testimonial from a respected source; or (f) to state falsely that product claims have been certified by a testing agency.

3. A NEW APPLICATION—The Supreme Court recently added to this list the creation in a television commercial of the false impression that the viewer is seeing a test, experiment, or demonstration of a product's qualities when, because of the undisclosed use of "mockups," the viewer is not seeing an actual test of the product photographed as performed. Even if the product will in fact pass the test and "mockups" are used only because of technical problems of photography, the Supreme Court could see no difference between this practice and the use of false testimonials or testing-agency certification.

4. LITERAL TRUTH SOMETIMES INSUFFICIENT—Advertisements are not intended to be carefully dissected with a dictionary at hand, but rather to produce an overall impression on the ordinary purchaser. An advertiser cannot present one overall impression yet protect himself by presenting a contrary impression in a small and inconspicuous portion of the advertisement. Even though every sentence considered separately is true, the advertisement as a whole may be misleading because factors are omitted or the message is composed in a misleading way. An advertisement that can be read to have two meanings is illegal if one of them is false or misleading.

5. KNOWLEDGE OF FALSITY AND INTENT—Because a basic purpose of the law is consumer protection, the government does not have to prove knowledge of falsity on the part of the advertiser; the businessman acts at his peril. The intent

162 LAW FOR EVERYONE

of the advertiser is also entirely immaterial. An advertiser may possess a wholly innocent intent and still violate the law.

Vicious Animals

1. THE OWNER'S RESPONSIBILITY — The owners of vicious animals are responsible for any injuries the animals may cause while running at large. If a dog annoys travelers on a public road by scaring horses or frightening children, the owner is responsible in damages to the injured party. The owner of a vicious bull or stallion is required to exercise the greatest care in protecting the public from injury. If a person on a social or business errand is injured by a savage animal on the premises of the owner, the owner is responsible.

2. TRESPASSERS — These rules do not apply to trespassers who know the dangerous nature of the animal.

3. DOMESTIC ANIMALS — The owner of domestic animals is responsible in case injury results because of his own negligence. On the other hand, if the animals trespass on a neighbor's land, they cannot be injured or killed by the neighbor. The neighbor has a legal remedy, however, and can collect damages.

4. FENCE LAWS — In certain sections of the country there are open lands where cattle and other animals are allowed to graze at will. The owners of cultivated land are there required to provide their own protection against the animals. Most states, however, have stock laws providing that animals must be kept within an enclosure, and if damage results the owner of the animals is responsible.

Wills

1. DEFINITIONS — A *will* or *testament* is generally a written instrument making disposition of a person's property, to take effect after his death. A *testator* is the maker of a will when the same is made by a male person; if a female, the maker is called a *testatrix*. A *codicil* is an addition or alteration of a part of an executed will. A *legacy* is a gift or bequest of money or personal property by will. The person to whom it is given is called a *legatee,* and if the gift consists of the remainder of the property after paying all debts and other legacies, he is called the *residuary legatee*. A person to whom real estate is given is called a *devisee*. An *executor* is a male person named in the will to whom is entrusted the duty of administrating the estate of the testator according to the

provisions of the will. If the will names a female person, she is called the *executrix*. An *administrator* is a male person appointed by the court to administer the estate of a deceased person who did not have a will or whose will named as executor a party incompetent or unwilling to act in that capacity. If the party appointed by the court is a female person, she is called the *administratrix*. Some states have abandoned terminology that distinguishes between the sexes, using *administrator* or *testator* for persons of either sex.

2. WHO MAY MAKE A WILL—All persons are competent to make wills except infants, persons of unsound mind, and idiots. In like manner any person who is competent to make a will can appoint his own executor. If the person so appointed is legally competent to transact business, the court will confirm the appointment if he lives within the jurisdiction of the court.

3. KINDS OF WILLS—There are two kinds of wills, written and unwritten. An unwritten will is called *nuncupative*. Such a will might be made by a soldier in active service or a sailor at sea, and depends upon proof of the persons hearing it.

4. REQUIREMENTS:
a. A will should be written.
b. A will should be dated.
c. Testator should sign his name in full, by mark if necessary.
d. A will should be witnessed by two or more disinterested parties, the number of witnesses varying according to statutes.
e. The witnesses need not know the contents of the will. It is generally necessary that the testator acknowledge to them that it is his will, sign it in their presence, and request them to sign as witnesses in his presence and in the presence of each other.
f. The wishes of the testator should be fully and clearly expressed in the will.
g. No exact form of words is necessary to make a will.
h. In writing wills simple language should be used. Statements concerning every provision or condition of the will should be fully and plainly made.
i. A will is valid even if written with a lead pencil.
j. To be effective in matters pertaining to real estate, a will must be executed according to the laws of the state in which the real estate is located. This requirement is generally in regard to the number of witnesses to a will. Care should be exercised to dispose of all the property belonging to the person making a will. In order to ac-

complish this, a will should have a clause, "all the rest, residue, and remainder of my estate, I give ..." etc., or "all the rest, residue, and remainder of my estate shall be divided into the following parts, 1/3 to ......, 1/6 to ......," etc.

k. Personal property may be conveyed in accordance with the law of the state in which the testator resides.

l. If trust provisions or limited estates are to be provided for in a will, it is best to have the will drawn by a competent lawyer, as these provisions are very technical, and may result in much litigation if not carefully drawn.

m. Generally a person does not need to give his property or any part of it to his children, but mention of the names of all the children is evidence of the testator's competency.

5. CODICILS — The same principles apply to a codicil as to a will. A codicil must be signed in the presence of witnesses.

6. MARRIED WOMEN — A wife is entitled to a certain portion of her husband's property called the dower. If the will does not provide that amount for her, she can have it set aside and claim her dower right.

7. A WILL IS SET ASIDE under the following conditions:

a. When it can be proved that the testator was feeble-minded or lacking in mental capacity.

b. When the testator revokes it before death, in which case it is usually destroyed.

c. When the property devised has been disposed of during the testator's lifetime.

8. GENERAL PRINCIPLES:

a. Any person may be a devisee or a legatee, including married women, minors, or corporations.

b. Testator's property is primarily liable for testator's debts and funeral expenses, which must be paid before any part of the property can be distributed to legatees.

c. A will has no force or effect until after testator's death.

d. The last will annuls all former wills.

e. A will takes effect from the day of the testator's death.

f. All matters pertaining to wills and inheritances are handled by the court having probate jurisdiction.

9. EXECUTORS AND ADMINISTRATORS — An executor is named in a will to execute that will and settle the estate. If the will does not name an executor, or if the named executor will not or cannot act, the probate court, in some states called the surrogate court, in others orphans' court, appoints an administrator with the will annexed. If a person dies without leaving a will, the court appoints an administrator, whose duty is the same as that of an executor except

that he, having no will of the deceased, distributes the property as the law directs. The duties of an executor are:

a. To see that the deceased is suitably buried, avoiding unreasonable expense if the estate is insolvent.

b. To offer the will for probate, or proving, and to conform to the laws of his state and rules of the court, the clerk of which will give full instructions.

c. To make and return to the court within required time an inventory of the property. Real estate lying in another state need not be inventoried, for that must be administered upon in the state where it lies; but personal property situated in another state should be inventoried. Any encumbrances upon real estate should be noted and described.

d. To collect the property, pay the debts and dispose of the remainder as the law and will, or either, directs. Generally the debts should be paid as follows: (1) funeral expenses, (2) expenses of last sickness, (3) debts due the United States, (4) debts due the state, and (5) claims of creditors.

e. To render the accounts as directed by the court. The law provides that the widow of the intestate shall be the first entitled to act as administrator; next, the nearest of kin who is competent; next, any creditor who will accept the trust; and lastly, any other suitable person. Executors and administrators are required to take an official oath and also to give bond, usually for double the amount of the estate. Any blanks for probate may usually be secured from the clerk of the court having probate jurisdiction.

   10. FORM OF WILL—To be valid, a will must be in writing and signed at the end by the testator in the presence of at least two witnesses or, in some jurisdictions, three witnesses, who must all be present when the testator signs his name to the will. The witnesses must also sign their names as such witnesses in the presence of each other and in the presence of the testator. If the will is written on more than one single sheet, it is a wise precaution for the testator and all of the witnesses to sign their names on each sheet.

WILL FORM

I, ..., residing in . . . ., in the County of . . . ., and State of . . . ., being of sound mind and disposing memory do make, ordain, publish, and declare this to be my Last Will and Testament, hereby revoking all former Wills and Codicils by me made.

|Here insert all bequests and instructions|

Lastly, I make, constitute, and appoint ....
to be the executor(trix) of this my Last Will and Testament.

In witness whereof, I have hereunto subscribed my name and affixed my seal the ...... day of ...., in the year of Our Lord, One Thousand Nine Hundred and ....

.... (Seal)

Testator's Signature

This instrument was on the day of the date hereof, signed, published, and declared by the said testator .... to be his (her) Last Will and Testament in the presence of us who at his (her) request have subscribed our names hereto as witnesses, in his (her) presence, and in the presence of each other.

|Witnesses' names and addresses|

GLOSSARY OF LEGAL TERMS

abrogate. To repeal or set aside a statute or ruling.

access. The right to enter and leave a tract of land from a public way.

acknowledgment. A sworn statement that a legal document was executed by the person making the acknowledgment. The statement is made before a public official, who attaches a certificate of acknowledgment to the document.

administrator. A person appointed by a probate court to settle the affairs of an individual dying without a will.

ad valorem. Designates an assessment of taxes against property according to value.

affidavit. A voluntary written statement of fact sworn before an authorized public official.

agent. A person authorized to represent another person and conduct business transactions in his name.

amortization. The act or process of extinguishing a debt, usually with equal payments at regular intervals over a specific period of time.

ancillary. Designating or pertaining to a document, proceeding, officer or office, etc., that is subordinate to, or in aid of, another primary or principal one; as, an ancillary attachment, bill or suit presupposes the existence of another principal proceeding.

annuity. A sum of money or its equivalent that constitutes one of a series of periodic payments. Any advance that may be interpreted in terms of money and answers the requirements of regularity may be considered an annuity.

antitrust law. A body of law designed to prevent corporations or conglomerates from developing monopoly power or unlawful combinations.

appraisal. An estimate of quantity, quality or value. The process through which conclusions of property value or property facts are obtained; also commonly the report setting forth such estimate and conclusion.

assessment. A non-recurring charge levied against property to meet some specific purpose portioned either by benefit derived to property or based on value of property. The valuation of property for taxation; also the value so assigned.

assets. Property of all kinds under a single ownership.

auctioneer. A person employed for compensation to sell property to the highest bidder at a public sale.

authenticate. To give authority to a

legal document so it may be used as evidence in a court of law. Notaries public and other public officials are empowered to authenticate documents.

avoid. To set aside or make void.

B

bailment. A temporary transfer of personal property for some specific purpose. The property is to be returned after the purpose has been executed.

bankruptcy. The legally declared condition of being unable to pay one's debts.

bill of exchange. An unconditional order in writing from one person to another directing that a certain sum of money be paid to a third person; sometimes called a *draft*.

bill of sale. A legal paper transferring title to personal property from one person to another.

blue sky law. A popular name for a law designed to regulate and supervise the issuance and selling of securities.

bond. 1. A legal instrument binding a person to pay a specific sum of money to another person at a specified time. **2.** A certificate of obligation, usually an evidence of debt.

broker. A person who conducts transactions in his specialized field.

C

capital. Accumulated wealth. A portion of wealth which is set aside for the production of additional wealth; specifically, the funds belonging to the partners or shareholders of a business, invested with the expressed intention of their remaining permanently in the business.

carrier. A person whose business is to transport passengers or merchandise.

certificate of title. A document usually given to the home buyer with the deed stating that title to the property is clear; it is prepared by a title company or an attorney and is based on the abstract of title.

chancery. Equity. A *master in chancery* is an assistant to the judge in a court of equity.

chattel. Any item of movable or immovable property other than real estate.

chattel mortgage. An instrument conveying conditional title to personal property as security for the repayment of a debt or for the performance of some other act.

citizen. An inhabitant of a nation who enjoys political rights.

class action suit. A lawsuit filed on behalf of all people who find themselves in the same factual situation.

clear title. A title which is not encumbered or burdened with defects.

codicil. An addition to or modification of a will. A codicil requires the same formalities as a will.

collateral. Any property designated as security for the payment of a debt or for the execution of a contract.

commercial paper. Negotiable instruments, such as checks, bills of exchange, or bank notes given as unconditional payment in business transactions.

commission. Payment for the performance of specific duties; in real estate, usually payment measured by a percentage of another sum, i.e., as a percentage of the sales price paid for selling a property.

common property. Land or a tract of land considered as the property of the public in which all persons enjoy equal rights; property not owned by individuals or government, but by groups or in formal villages.

complaint. The initial statement made by the plaintiff in a civil case, stating the reasons the plaintiff is entitled to the aid of the court.

compound interest. Interest paid both on the original principal and on interest accrued from the time it fell due.

condemnation. The taking of private property for public use through the exercising of due process of law.

condominium. A form of property ownership providing for individual ownership of a specific apartment together with an undivided interest in the land or other parts of the structure in common with other owners.

consideration. That which a party to a contract gains from the contract; any valuable benefit gained by the signer of a contract. No contract is valid unless it expresses a consideration.

consignee. A person to whom goods are shipped or transferred.

contempt of court. Violation of the rules of a court of law or disruption of its proceedings.

contingent claim. A claim against a person that is conditional on some event that may not happen. Contingent claims are not allowable in bankruptcy proceedings.

contract. A mutual agreement between two or more competent parties who, for a valuable consideration, assent to do or not to do a particular thing.

convey. The act of deeding or transferring title to another.

conveyance. A written legal document transferring title to real property from one person to another.

copyright. The exclusive right to sell, reproduce, or use in any way a literary or artistic work.

corporation. 1. An association of persons created under the law and legally empowered to act as a single person in regard to some common purpose of the members. **2.** A group of persons empowered to act as a single individual, and treated as such, in many respects, by the law.

covenant. An agreement written into deeds and other instruments promising performance or nonperformance of certain acts or stipulating certain uses or nonuses of the property.

crime. A wrong which violates a statute and injures or endangers the public.

curtesy. The interest which a husband acquires in land belonging to his wife after her death; sometimes called *dower.*

D

debenture. An instrument, given by a corporation to certain investors, promising to repay their investments with interest, securing the debts with company assets, and giving the investors priority claims.

deed. A written document conveying real estate from one owner to another.

default. Failure to carry out a legally binding promise.

defeasance. A provision or condition in a deed or in a separate instrument which, being performed, renders the instrument void.

demand draft. A draft drawn by one person on another which is payable when presented.

demurrage. The sum charged by transportation companies for goods not removed from their cars within a fixed time.

deposition. The sworn testimony of a witness taken down in writing before a notary public and signed by the witness.

devise. A gift of real property by last will and testament.

devisee. A person given real estate by a will.

discrimination. Any act which denies rights or equal treatment to a person because of race, color, religion, or sex.

docketing. Scheduling a case to be heard before a court of justice.

domicile. The permanent home of a person. Temporary homes are *residences*.

double indemnity. An agreement in a life insurance or accident policy providing for payment of twice the value of the policy in case of accidental death.

dower. The provision the law makes to support a widow out of her deceased spouse's estate.

draft. A written order by one person on another demanding the payment of a specified sum of money to a designated third person.

drunkenness. The state of being so influenced by alcohol that judgment and reflexes are impaired.

E

easement. The right to use or enjoy certain privileges that appertain to the land of another such as the right of way, or the right to receive air and light by reason of an agreement of record with the owner of adjacent property.

ejectment. An action to determine the title to land and right of possession.

emancipation. The release of control by a parent over a minor.

embezzlement. The use of another person's money or property for one's own benefit by a person such as an agent, an executor, or a public official.

eminent domain. The power to appropriate private property for public use. If public welfare is served, the right of eminent domain may be granted by the state to quasi-public or even private bodies such as railroad, water, light and power companies.

encumbrance. Any claim, such as a mortgage or a lien, against a piece of real or personal property.

endorsement. The signature of the owner on the back of a check or other negotiable instrument, by which he transfers the instrument to another person.

equity. 1. Equity of redemption. **2.** A body of laws supplementing and overriding the limitations and inflexibility of common law.

equity of redemption. The right of a mortgagor to redeem his property within a certain time after foreclosure.

escheat. Reversion of property to the state by reason of failure of persons legally entitled to hold or lack of heirs.

escrow. A deed or other instrument placed in the hands of a disinterested person (sometimes called the *escrowee)* for delivery upon performance of certain conditions or the happening of certain contingencies.

estate. A right in property. An *estate in land* is the degree, nature or extent of interest which a person has in it.

evidence. Any statement or object presented in court to convince the judge or jury of the truth of an argument.

execution. The completion or fulfillment of anything, such as a contract. An *executed contract* is one whose terms have already been completed.

exemption. A right granted to debtors that protects certain property from the claims of creditors.

F

fee. Remuneration for services. When applied to property, an inheritable estate in land.

fiduciary. The relationship between a person charged with the duty of acting for the benefit of another, as between guardian and ward.

forced sale. The act of selling property under compulsion as to time and place. Usually a sale made by virtue of a court order, ordinarily at public auction.

foreclosure. Taking mortgaged property from an owner who fails to pay the debt secured by the mortgage.

forfeiture. A statement entitling a landlord to terminate a lease and reclaim property if a tenant fails to pay rent.

franchise. A privilege or right conferred by governmental grant or contractually by a business enterprise upon an individual or group of individuals. Usually, an exclusive privilege or right to furnish public services or sell a particular product in a certain community.

G

guaranteed mortgage. A mortgage in which a mortgage company buys the mortgages with its own funds and in turn sells these mortgages to its clients, who receive all of the papers in connection with the mortgage, including the bond, the mortgage and the assignment, together with the company's policy of guarantee. The company guarantees the payment of both principal and interest and assumes the responsibility of complete supervision of the mortgage, for which it receives a fee out of the interest, as it is collected.

guaranty. A written promise by one party to perform some duty or pay some debt if another party should fail to do so.

guaranty policy. Insurance that protects the buyer from loss due to any defect in title to a piece of real property.

H

habeas corpus. A writ ordering a law enforcement officer to bring a certain prisoner into court and show legal reasons to keep him in custody.

heir. One who might inherit or succeed to an interest in lands under the rules of law, applicable where an individual dies without leaving a will.

I

indemnify. To protect from loss or damage, especially by agreeing to reimburse a person for certain kinds of loss.

indemnity. Repayment by an insurer for a loss the insured person has suffered.

indenture. A type of written instrument in which both parties agree to do certain things.

infant. A person too young, in the eyes of the law, to manage his own affairs and enjoy full rights of citizenship; a minor.

injunction. A court order forbidding a person or his associates from doing or continuing to do certain actions.

innkeeper. The proprietor of a public house that receives and entertains travelers.

insolvency. Inability of a person or business to pay his or its debts.

instrument. A formal legal document.

insurance. A contract stating that one person will compensate another for certain specific kinds of losses.

interlocutory decree. An intermediate or temporary ruling of a court, not a final decision of a case.

international law. A body of rules governing the conduct of nations.

intestate. A person who dies without leaving a valid last will and testament.

J

jury. A body of laymen selected impartially to determine the truth in a legal proceeding.

L

lease. A contract for the possession or occupancy of land or buildings.

legacy. A gift left by means of a will to a named person, who is called the *legatee*. The *residuary legatee* is the person named to receive all property not specifically given to someone else.

lessee. One who possesses the right to use or occupy a property under lease agreement.

lessor. One who holds title to and conveys the right to use and occupy a property under lease agreement.

letters patent. The legal document granting a patent to an inventor.

liable. Legally responsible. The law will force a person to pay for damage he is liable for.

license. A permission granted by a competent authority allowing a person to do something that he would otherwise have no right to do.

lien. The right to hold or sell the property of another person as security or for the payment of a debt.

liquidated. 1. Set or determined. A liquidated debt is for a specific amount. **2.** Settled by payment or other means, as a debt.

liquidated damages clause. A statement in a contract setting a monetary penalty for violation of the contract.

litigation. 1. A legal action for the purpose of enforcing a law. **2.** The undertaking of legal action.

M

mandamus. A command from a court to a public or private official requiring him to do some act that is his official duty.

material. Important. A material fact influences the decision of the court.

mechanic's lien. A claim against a piece of property to insure payment for labor or materials used in building or reparing the property.

repairing the property.

Medicare. A federal program of health insurance for the aged.

monument. A stone or other fixed object used to establish real estate boundaries.

mortgage. An agreement designating certain property as security for the payment of a debt.

motion. 1. In parliamentary law, a formal proposal to be considered by a meeting. **2.** An application to a court for a rule or other order.

municipal corporation. A corporation formed to govern a town or a city.

N

negotiable instrument. Any legal document which may be transferred by endorsement.

notary public. A public official empowered by law to administer oaths and to attest writings for the purpose of establishing their authenticity.

note. An instrument of credit given to attest a debt.

nuncupative will. A will made orally, in the presence of several witnesses, during the testator's last illness.

O

obligation. A conditional bond agreeing to pay a certain sum of money if the signer fails to do a specified thing.

option. An agreement granting the exclusive right during a stated period of time, without creating any obligation to purchase, sell or otherwise direct or contract the use of a property.

ordinance. A regulation passed by a municipal government.

P

parliamentary law. The generally accepted rules of procedure for public meetings or deliberative bodies.

partnership. An association of two or more persons to carry on as coowners of a business for profit.

passport. An official document of identification given to travelers to prove their citizenship.

patent. The exclusive right to manufacture and sell an invention, granted to its inventor for a limited time.

personalty. Property which is movable. All property is either personalty, realty or mixed.

plaintiff. The person who sues another in civil court.

power of attorney. A legal document by one person authorizing another person to act for him in certain specified matters.

power of sale. A clause inserted in a will or deed of trust agreement authorizing the sale or transfer of land in accordance with the terms of the clause.

prescriptive right. A legal right acquired by uninterrupted use of the right over a long period of time.

principal. 1. A sum lent or employed as a fund or investment, as distinguished from its income or profits. 2. The original amount (as of a loan) of the total due and payable at a certain date. 3. A party to a transaction, as distinguished from an agent. 4. Head of a business.

privileged communication. A confidential statement to a trusted person such as a doctor, lawyer, priest, or spouse; these persons are not allowed to reveal that information in court.

products liability. The liability of a manufacturer or seller of a product for any injury to a consumer using the product for its intended purposes.

property. The exclusive right to control an economic good. The recognized attribute that human beings may have in their relation with wealth. A property refers to units capable of being used independently in a single ownership. A property may consist of the rights to a single parcel of land, a house and lot, a complete manufacturing plant or any one of the items assembled together to constitute such a plant. It may also consist of the rights developed and inherent in the attached business of an enterprise or any one of the elements reflected therein, such as the rights to a patent, a trademark, a contract or the proven goodwill of the public.

prorate. To allocate between seller and buyer their proportionate share of an obligation paid or due. For example, a prorate of real property taxes or fire insurance.

prospectus. A description of a company which invites the public to buy the securities of that company.

protest. A formal declaration, signed by a notary public, that a check or other negotiable instrument was presented for payment and that payment was denied.

proxy. A statement by a stockholder of a corporation appointing another person to vote in his place at stockholders' meetings.

putative father. The father of an illegitimate child.

Q

quitclaim deed. A deed transferring whatever interest the seller may have in a piece of real property. See also *warranty deed.*

R

real property. Land or anything permanently attached to it.

receiver. A person appointed by the court to hold and manage property that is involved in a lawsuit.

recording. The entering or recording

of a copy of certain legal instruments or documents, as a deed, in a government office provided for this purpose; thus making a public record of the document for the protection of all concerned and giving constructive notice to the public at large.

redeem. To gain full possession of property by paying off a mortgage or other obligation.

redemption. The recovery, by payment of all proper charges, of property which has been lost through foreclosure of a mortgage or other legal process.

release. A legal document by which one party in a dispute transfers its claim to another party.

release clause. A clause relinquishing a right or claim by the person in whom it exists to the person against whom it could be enforced; such as a clause in a mortgage deed reconveying the legal title to the mortgagor upon payment of the mortgage debt.

remise. A formal term meaning to give up.

replevin. A lawsuit to recover goods which have been illegally taken, usually goods taken to secure payment of rent.

S

seal. A formal marking or stamp on a legal document; now rarely used.

secure. To guarantee that a debt will be paid by giving the creditor security, such as a lien or a mortgage. In bankruptcy, a secured claim is backed by some special right to the debtor's property.

secured credit sale. A sale in which the seller has the right to repossess the goods he sold if he is not fully paid.

securities. Any form of investment, including stocks, bonds, and notes. Also, property set aside to assure the payment of a debt.

security agreement. A contract signed by both buyer and seller stating that the seller has an interest in the goods until they are paid for.

specialty. A contract under seal, legally more binding than a simple contract.

squatter's right. The right to occupancy of land created by virtue of long and undisturbed use but without legal title or arrangement; in the nature of a right at common law.

statute. Any written law created by a legislature.

statute of limitations. A law stating that if a lawsuit is not begun within a specified time after a wrong occurred, the lawsuit becomes invalid.

statutory exemptions. Certain kinds of property that are protected by law from the claims of creditors.

statutory lien. A claim on property not in the creditor's possession, such as a mechanic's lien.

stoppage in transit. A right of the seller to reclaim goods before they are delivered to a purchaser if the goods are not paid for and if the purchaser is insolvent.

sublease. An agreement conveying the right of use and occupancy of a property in which the lessor is the lessee in a prior lease.

sue. To commence legal proceedings.

surety. A person who accepts final responsibility to fulfill another person's obligation if the other person should default.

surrogate court. A court that oversees the administration of wills.

T

tangible property. Property that by its nature is susceptible to the senses. Generally the land, fixed improvement, furnishings, merchandise, cash and other items of working capital used in carrying on an enterprise.

tenancy. A holding, as of land, by any kind of title, occupancy of land, a house or the like under a lease or on payment of rent or tenure.

tenancy in common. A tenancy shared by two or more parties.

tenant. Any person in possession of real property with the owner's permission.

time draft. A draft that is payable at a

specified time after it is presented.

title. Evidence that a person owns a piece of property. A merchantable title is entirely free from other claims of ownership.

tort. A wrong committed against an individual or his property independent of a contract.

trademark. A distinctive, legally registered marking or symbol used by manufacturers to distinguish their products.

W

warrant. 1. To assure a buyer that he will receive valid title to property, or to swear that facts stated in a contract are true. **2.** The act of a criminal court authorizing the arrest of a person or the search or seizure of property.

warranty. A statement relating to a sale of goods which assures the buyer that he will receive good quality merchandise.

warranty deed. A deed in which a seller of real estate guarantees that the title to the property is good.

will. A written declaration expressing a person's intention regarding the disposition of his property after his death.

without recourse. A phrase signifying a qualified endorsement—the signer denies liability for the negotiable instrument he endorses.